D0251078

Shaping the
Game

Shaping the
Game

The New Leader's Guide
to Effective Negotiating

Michael Watkins

Harvard Business School Press

Boston, Massachusetts

Copyright 2006 Michael Watkins
All rights reserved
Printed in the United States of America
10 09 08 07 06   5 4 3 2

No part of this publication may be reproduced, stored in or introduced
into a retrieval system, or transmitted, in any form, or by any means
(electronic, mechanical, photocopying, recording, or otherwise),
without the prior permission of the publisher. Requests for permission
should be directed to permissions@hbsp.harvard.edu, or mailed to
Permissions, Harvard Business School Publishing, 60 Harvard Way,
Boston, Massachusetts 02163.

978-1-4221-0252-7 (ISBN 13)

Library of Congress Cataloging-in-Publication Data

Watkins, Michael, 1956–
    Shaping the game : the new leader's guide to effective negotiating /
Michael Watkins.
        p. cm.
    Includes bibliographical references.
    ISBN 1-4221-0252-1
1. Communication in management.   2. Negotiation.   3. Problem solving.
4. Persuasion (Psychology)   5. Executive ability.   I. Title.
HD30.3.W38 2006
658.4'052—dc22   2006000452

The paper used in this publication meets the minimum requirements of
the American National Standard for Information Sciences—Permanence
of Paper for Printed Library Materials, ANSI Z39.48-1992.

To Shawna, and to our children,

Aidan, Maeve, and Niall

Contents

3. Match Strategy to Situation   57

The dangers of one-size-fits-all thinking. The need to match your negotiation style to the type of situation you face. How to diagnose negotiations and develop high-impact strategies.

4. Plan to Learn and Influence   97

The need to learn and influence in interactions with counterparts. Figuring out what you need to learn and how to learn it. Shaping counterparts' perceptions of their interests and alternatives.

5. Shape the Game   123

Skills that distinguish great negotiators from good ones. The critical importance of having an early influence on who negotiates and what the agenda is. Strategies for shaping the game, both at and away from the table.

6. Organize to Improve   153

Learning as a sustainable source of competitive advantage. Accelerating your development as a negotiator. Evaluating negotiation training programs. Fostering organizational improvement in negotiation-intensive organizations.

Conclusion   175

The approach as a whole. Coordinating strategies to play and shape the game, and actions at and away from the table.

Preface

I wrote my book on accelerating transitions, *The First 90 Days*, because there was a big gap in the leadership literature. While many books have been written on the general subject of leadership, there was no good advice about how to accelerate transitions into new leadership roles. I hoped the book would do well. But I had no idea just how big a gap there was to fill. So it has been tremendously gratifying to find that so many leaders have benefited from reading *The First 90 Days* and applying its principles.

Why follow it up with a book on negotiation for new leaders? Because I've come to believe that success in transitioning and success in negotiating are inextricably linked. Long before I started writing about leadership transitions, I studied and taught negotiation. My work in this area influenced my thinking about how to help leaders get up to speed in their new roles. Beginning with my research on negotiation in new product development teams in the late 1980s, through six years in the early 1990s at the Kennedy School of Government studying the world's greatest diplomats, such as James Baker, Robert Gallucci, Richard Holbrooke, and Shimon Peres, and on to teaching negotiation at the Program on Negotiation at Harvard Law School and offering my Corporate Diplomacy course at the Harvard Business School, negotiation has been an abiding passion. So it was natural for me to incorporate negotiation thinking into my writing on leadership transitions. That's why there are chapters on "Negotiating Success" in relationships with new bosses, and "Creating Coalitions" to support key initiatives in *The First 90 Days*.

Since that book was published, I've had the opportunity to teach transition acceleration programs in leading companies worldwide and to engage with newly appointed managers in a wide range of industries and cultures. And I've found these managers are hungry for more, especially about navigating the myriad complex, high-stakes influence challenges that confront new leaders. In fact, the questions that I am most often asked by people who have read *The First 90 Days* are all about negotiation and its close cousins, influence and coalition building. "You've whetted my appetite," they say, "but where's the main course?" "How do I negotiate expectations and resources in my new role? How do I gain support for my early-win initiatives? How do I deal more effectively with powerful external and internal constituencies to lay a foundation for success?"

This book is my response to those questions. It delves deeply into key influence issues that were mentioned, but not adequately dealt with, in *The First 90 Days* and provides a framework and tools for dealing with them effectively. While the focus is on new leaders, the basic principles can be applied to a wide array of negotiating situations—from deciding where the family will go for summer vacation to negotiating the most complex merger deals.

So for those of you who feel at sea in new roles where your success rests on your effectiveness in negotiating, take heart!

—Michael Watkins
Newton, Massachusetts
January 2006

Acknowledgments

This book was inspired by the people who taught me how to think about negotiation. First and foremost is Howard Raiffa, the father of the field of negotiation analysis, my mentor, and my friend. It was Howard who taught me (or at least tried to teach me) how to take complex problems and distill them down to their strategic essence. Howard's work on decision analysis and negotiation analysis, especially his seminal work, *The Art and Science of Negotiation,* had an enormous influence on me.

Next is Jim Sebenius, a fellow intellectual son of Howard Raiffa. Jim embodies a rare and precious combination of the best that the academic world can offer—discipline, rigor, and creative insight—and the finest practical strategic mind I have had the privilege to encounter. With his coauthor, David Lax, Jim wrote a book, *The Manager as Negotiator,* and a series of articles that powerfully shaped my thinking about the subject. Jim also brought me from the Kennedy School of Government to the Harvard Business School and was a pillar of support for my work there.

Heartfelt thanks as well to my former colleagues at the Program on Negotiation at Harvard Law School, the Kennedy School

of Government, and the Harvard Business School, from whom
I have had the privilege to learn about the art and science of
negotiation: Marjorie Aaron, Max Bazerman, Joe Bower, Joel
Cutcher-Gershenfeld, Charan Devereaux, Roger Fisher, Brian
Hall, Robert Lawrence, Brian Mandell, Robert McKersie, Bruce
Patton, Hannah Riley, Jeswald Salacuse, Guhan Subramanian,
Malcolm Salter, Larry Susskind, William Ury, Paul Vaalor,
Richard Walton, and Michael Wheeler.

I also am deeply indebted to the skilled practitioners who
have graciously shared their practical insights and reflections
with me, especially Robert Aiello, James Baker, John Eckert,
Peter Galbraith, Robert Gallucci, Quentin Heim, Richard Holbrooke, Steven Holtzman, and Shimon Peres. They are great
negotiators in every sense of the word.

Finally, I would never have started studying leadership transitions, and the role of negotiation in them, if Dan Ciampa hadn't
encouraged me. Our experience in writing *Right from the Start*
not only got me interested in the subject, it initiated me into the
wonderful world of book writing. For that experience, and for
the friendship that resulted, I will always be grateful.

Introduction

L EADERSHIP IS ULTIMATELY about leverage. To
lead, you must figure out how to tap into the
sources of potential energy that are latent in your
organization, and powerfully channel them to achieve desired
goals. After all, you are just one person; alone, you can achieve
little.

The essence of leadership, then, lies first in identifying sources
of potential energy—in the people, relationships, technologies,
products, systems, and structures in your organization—and
then in figuring out how to activate and align them. Great leaders catalyze action; they serve as the template for driving alignment and creating a sense of purpose in the seeming chaos and
complexity of human organization.

While difficult for established leaders, the challenge of leveraging oneself to create powerful new patterns of activity is particularly acute for leaders entering new roles. Why? Because
when you enter a new leadership role, you typically lack knowledge of what sources of potential energy are available to you. You
also don't know what goals are desirable and feasible to achieve;
until you figure that out, you can't mobilize yourself and others

1

to pursue them. Critically, you lack the relationships with other influential people in the organization necessary to gain their commitment and support.

In the decade that I have spent studying leadership transitions and helping leaders accelerate themselves into new roles, my views about what is really critical have shifted considerably. Early on, I believed that new leaders gained leverage by putting in place the right *strategies, structures, and systems.* I approached transitions as an engineer would approach a challenging design problem, advising leaders to identify the right goals, develop a supporting strategy, align the architecture of the organization, and figure out what projects to pursue to secure early wins.

As my understanding of the realities confronting leaders in transition deepened, however, I came to believe that *relationships* are just as important, if not more so, sources of leverage. This realization elevated relationships, and the energy they can mobilize (or drain from you), to the forefront of my thinking about how to help leaders enter and gain momentum in challenging new roles.

This is not to say, of course, that strategies, structures, and systems are unimportant; usually they are critical. But if you hope to put in place the right strategies, structures, and systems, you must first secure victory on the relationship front. This means building credibility with influential players, gaining agreement with them on goals, and securing their commitment to devote their energies to helping you achieve those goals. Leverage through relationships is an essential foundation for effectiveness in a new leadership role.

Put another way, I have come to believe that negotiation is the single most important skill that leaders exercise during their transitions into new roles. By *negotiation,* incidentally, I don't mean haggling over a used car; I mean a more expansive view of

negotiation as *creating and capturing value in a network of relationships*.[1] As we will discuss in detail later, this view of negotiation
focuses attention on how new leaders can reach agreements (formal or tacit) with other influential players in order to pursue
mutually beneficial ends. It also highlights the importance of
investing to build and sustain those critical relationships.

Where, you might well be asking at this point, does authority
fit into the picture for leaders in transition? Why so much emphasis on influence and so little on formal authority? Because
authority, in the traditional sense of a leader's position granting
them the rights to make certain important decisions and to
direct people to act in desired ways, is in very short supply these
days. Flatter organizations and matrix structures have dramatically diminished its importance. In fact, new leaders who believe
that their positions grant them the authority to make substantial changes tend to get themselves into hot water very quickly.
You would be wise to view authority—or equivalently, the mandate to make change happen in your new organization—
as something to be painstakingly built and sustained through
the creation of a network of agreements with other influential
players.

The basic theme of this book, then, is that effective leaders
negotiate their way to success in their new roles. Because if you
can't engage in effective negotiation (and its close relatives,
influence and alliance building), the best analysis and planning
isn't going to take you anywhere. The key drivers of effectiveness in your new role—gaining alignment with your new boss,
restructuring and leveraging your team, creating coalitions to
support your early-win initiatives, and dealing with customers
and suppliers—all boil down to negotiating effectively with influential players inside and outside your new organization. And
the importance of negotiating effectively increases the higher

you go, in part because your decisions have greater impact, and in part because you have to deal with more, and more powerful, players.

Negotiating a New Leadership Role

To illustrate the challenges of negotiating a leadership transition, let's consider the challenges facing Paul, an experienced manager preparing to take on a new role. When we first encounter Paul (we will return to his story throughout the book), he is negotiating with three potential employers about taking on the role of vice president of sales. While it may seem that Paul's negotiations *for* his new job and his negotiations once *in* the new position are not linked, nothing could be further from the truth. Paul's reputation and relationships will be strongly shaped by his interactions with his future bosses during the recruiting process. His employment negotiations inevitably will also deal with performance expectations and the resources he will have to work with in his new role. The understandings that result from this prehire dialogue will set the stage for everything that happens once Paul formally takes his new position. Seeing the situation in this light, he began negotiating his transition the moment he considered taking a new job.

Paul has worked hard to lay the groundwork for success in a sales executive role. After college, he earned his spurs as a top-flight representative in two companies. Recognizing his abilities, his current company promoted him to sales manager with assignments in increasingly large and important districts. Then he spent some time in marketing to learn the ropes. Three years ago, he was appointed director of sales for the company's largest region. Now, with almost a decade of experience, he feels ready to lead the sales function at a midsize company.

Concluding that opportunities were limited at his current company, Paul put himself on the market. After intensive research and numerous calls with recruiters, he narrowed the field to three companies—let's call them Alpha, Beta, and Gamma. Alpha is the largest of the three and the most successful. It also has a history of promoting salespeople with the right aptitude into senior executive positions, which is something to which Paul aspires. If he gets the job, he will be leading the sales function in Alpha's second-largest division, a very strong player in its industry. So the Alpha opportunity offers Paul the chance to work with an organization with a history of success and a record of developing leaders, and the chance to move up if he succeeds.

All else being equal, Alpha is Paul's first choice. He has gone through several rounds of interviews there, but the inside recruiter hasn't yet made him an offer. Paul assumes the company is talking with several candidates and hasn't decided which to offer the job to first.

Beta Corporation is somewhat smaller than Alpha and substantially less successful. In fact, it's essentially in turnaround mode. The previous VP of sales was recently let go, but the CEO has acknowledged that the problems go well beyond the sales function; he has been moving aggressively to reorient the company. Paul would be the VP of sales for the entire organization, so he would be able to run the whole show without interference from a corporate headquarters like Alpha's. He also is energized by the opportunity to participate in a turnaround, sensing that it could be a chance to really make his mark. At the same time, he's worried about the downside impact on his future prospects if things don't go well. Who wants to be known for helping to run a turnaround into the ground? Paul doesn't have an offer from Beta yet, but believes it would make him one if he pushed the process along a bit.

Finally, Gamma is Paul's "safety school." It's a smaller, well-managed company that would be delighted to have him; it's already made him an offer. Since it's a smaller company, Paul would be able to have an impact at Gamma far beyond the sales function, and this could help position him for future general management responsibility. This is assuming, however, that Gamma's owner doesn't turn out to be a control freak, a prospect about which Paul has some reason to worry. Also, the compensation package on offer is substantially below what he is confident he could get from Beta or Alpha, and it's unlikely he will be able to get Gamma to sweeten it much.

Paul's initial transition negotiation challenge, then, concerns which company he should seek to join and how he should approach negotiating the best possible package. Once he is in his new position, Paul will have to engage in numerous other negotiations, as illustrated in figure I-1, in a network of constituencies whose support will be critical to his success. As he strives to create momentum in the early months in his new job, he will have to:

- Further negotiate expectations and resources with his new boss (or bosses).

- Build relationships and negotiate for support and resources with his peers.

- Establish goals, expectations, and incentives with his direct reports and the entire sales organization.

- Gain support from influential people (such as the corporate headquarters in Alpha, and the CEOs of Beta or Gamma) for some major change initiatives.

- Repair some strained relationships and close major deals with key customers.

If he negotiates these challenges effectively, Paul will establish himself in his new role and lay the foundation for still greater success. If he doesn't, he could dig himself into a hole from which it will be hard to escape. In short, Paul's success in his new role will depend critically on his ability to navigate these and a host of other negotiating challenges during the first critical months in his new role.

Navigating by the North Star

The starting point for Paul, and for you if you are in transition, is to cultivate the right mind-set about negotiating your way into a new leadership role. You can't hope to negotiate effectively if

FIGURE I-1

New-leader negotiations

you aren't pursuing the right objectives. This means being clear in your own mind about your goals and methods, about the ends you will pursue and the means you will use (and not use) to achieve them.

What should Paul be trying to accomplish in the negotiations he undertakes with his potential employers and in the first few critical months in his new role? Given those goals, what should he do and what should he not do to achieve them?

Through my studies of hundreds of leaders in transition, I have come to believe that there are four fundamental objectives that new leaders should seek to achieve in every negotiation they undertake. Together, they provide the equivalent of a "north star" to guide new leaders' actions. If you keep your eye on them, you won't lose your way. So I would counsel you to approach all the negotiations you undertake during your transition seeking to achieve these goals:

1. **To create value to the greatest extent possible.** This means working tirelessly from the very first moments of your transition to identify the potential for mutual gains in the many relationships—inside your organization and with key external constituencies—that are key to your success. It also means identifying alignments of interest that can help you, and those with whom you seek to collaborate, to tap sources of potential energy and channel them to achieve desired goals.

2. **To capture an appropriate share of the value that gets created.** This means being sure that the agreements you enter into with other influential players really do advance your agenda. After all, you have important goals that you are trying to achieve. While it can be rewarding to help others, you can't afford to be too

altruistic. You need to set and enforce boundaries, lest your energy end up being harnessed too much to helping others achieve their ends at the expense of your own.

3. **To build and sustain critical relationships.** This means not trying to capture so much value in your negotiations that you sour relationships. It also means being careful not to exert influence in ways that are perceived to be self-serving or manipulative. Relationships are hard to build and easy to damage. Trust is particularly hard won. Once lost, it can be difficult or impossible to regain.

4. **To enhance your personal credibility.** This means establishing your reputation as a *tough, creative, and trustworthy* negotiator. It also means viewing every negotiation you undertake, inside and outside your organization, as an opportunity to build and reinforce your reputation. A good reputation is a priceless asset for a leader in transition; you must strive to build and sustain it in every interaction.

Arguably, this is good advice for all leaders, regardless of their situations. But the particular challenges confronting leaders in transition elevate these four north-star goals to the level of make-or-break imperatives. Why? Because new leaders usually have little or no capital—in terms of relationships and reputation—upon which they can draw. A well-established leader might be able to take some chances and put some capital in jeopardy by pushing the boundaries in terms of goals and methods. But new leaders can ill afford to take actions that have the potential to sour relationships or negatively influence the opinions of key constituencies at the outset. People form opinions of new leaders based on remarkably little data. Once formed, they are difficult or impossible to change.

For each of the four north-star goals, there are corresponding traps into which you can fall. Being good at capturing value but not at creating it can leave you battling over slices of very small pies. Negotiators can get so focused on not being "had" that they end up in a defensive crouch, unable to cooperate in order to create joint value. All too often, new leaders, because they feel vulnerable in their new roles, focus too much on playing defense. They jealously guard the resources they have and fail to be open to the many opportunities that surround them to create mutual gains.

Being good at creating value but not capturing it can leave you watching others devour the meal you cooked. Steven Holtzman, who built two successful pharmaceutical companies through inspired deal making, attributed his success to his ability to balance value creation and value capture: "First you have to establish that there is a valuable thing you could make together, 'a bucket of gold.' But then you must shift to a dialogue of 'Gentlemen, we really need to establish whether we are in the same ballpark in terms of monetary expectations.'"[2] The same basic principle holds in all the negotiations undertaken during transitions into new leadership roles. It's not enough to be good at creating value with others; you must be able capture and channel a reasonable amount of that value to achieve your own goals.

Failing to focus on relationships can leave you isolated, a potentially fatal condition for a new leader. Good business relationships, while not ends in their own right, are essential lubricants for ongoing dealings. They create reservoirs of goodwill upon which you can, judiciously, draw in times of need. They open up opportunities for mutually beneficial trades across time ("I'll give you a break on delivery this time if you give me a break on pricing next time") and risk-sharing arrangements ("You need to lock in a minimum financial return, and I'm willing to give you that in return for more of the upside"). Driving deals that are too favorable for you can leave counterparts bitter, disinclined to energetically implement agreements, and looking for payback the next time. If you are overseeing people negotiating on behalf of you or your organizations, you should likewise take care that their incentives don't encourage them to kill the goose just to bring home a few more golden eggs by the end of the quarter.

Finally, your reputation as a negotiator is hard to build, easy to lose, and difficult to recover. You can't go far wrong in building your reputation if you strive to be seen as tough, creative, and trustworthy. The creative part will help you open up opportunities for joint gain. The trustworthy part will help you sustain relationships. The tough part will help you capture your fair share of the value you create and immunize you against the hard bargainers. Remember, you must capture value on a sustainable basis, as well as create it. As Robert Gallucci, the accomplished American diplomat, so aptly put it, "Great negotiators never lose sight of what they are aiming at, which is not an agreement per se, but a desired outcome . . . Getting to yes is easy, all you have to do is roll over. It's getting what you want that's hard."[3]

What are the immediate implications for Paul and other leaders in transition? He should never lose sight of the fact that his prospective employers will decide whether to hire him, in no small measure, on the basis of how well he conducts these negotiations. They rightly will be asking, "What does the way he approaches these negotiations tell us about how he will conduct himself with bosses, peers, direct reports, customers, suppliers, and other key constituencies if we hire him?" So Paul has a Goldilocks problem. Negotiate too hard and they will wonder, "Is he too tough?" Don't negotiate hard enough and they will wonder, "Is he too soft?" If he negotiates in ways that are consistent with the four north-star goals, it will help him get it just right.

In sum, your negotiation goals during the transition into your new leadership role are to create value to the maximum degree possible, to capture value to the maximum extent that is sustainable, while carefully tending to key relationships, and preserving your reputation. Does that seem pretty straightforward? It is. But the devil is in the details, in *how* you approach negotiating to achieve these goals.

Overview of the Book

The rest of this book will provide you with the strategies and tools you need to excel in negotiating your new leadership role. The next chapter provides an essential vocabulary for analyzing the many negotiations that you will undertake. It will arm you with tools to understand the structure of negotiations and to shape the dynamics of negotiation processes.

Building on this foundation, chapter 2 lays out a framework for crafting strategies in order to achieve your north-star negotiation goals. It develops four key imperatives that will guide your strategy-development efforts:

- Match your strategy to the situation

- Learn about and influence your counterparts

- Shape the negotiation "games" you play

- Organize to learn from every negotiation you undertake

Subsequent chapters explore each of these four strategic imperatives in depth. Chapter 3 details how to *match strategy to situation*, by translating your diagnosis of the types of negotiations you are facing into the right strategies for creating and capturing value. It highlights crucial differences among various types of negotiations, and the need to adjust your approach accordingly. There is a world of difference, for example, between negotiating one-on-one with your boss over expectations and resources, and negotiating with many other influential players over initiating a significant organizational change. In the latter situation, it may be critical for you to focus on building alliances with particularly influential players, while in the negotiation with your boss alliances might be less relevant.

Chapter 4 highlights the need to both *learn and shape the perceptions* of the people with whom you negotiate. It provides detailed advice on how to approach these two essential tasks, exploring how you can better elicit valuable information from counterparts—for example, about their interests—and how you can more effectively frame what is at stake for them in ways that highlight potential joint gains. This chapter also underscores the importance of understanding how your counterparts perceive their alternatives, and working to influence how they see their choices.

Chapter 5 focuses on what you can do to *shape the game,* by influencing the structure of the negotiations in which you participate. Shaping the game means not passively sitting by while others define who participates, what the issues are, and what deadlines drive action. Great advantage in negotiations goes to the parties who define the rules of the game. The best negotiators never cede this advantage to others.

Finally, chapter 6 highlights the value to be realized by *organizing to learn* and get better at negotiating, both individually and for full organizations. While inborn abilities do shape one's potential to be a great negotiator, they are not determinative. The great negotiators I have been privileged to know invariably served long apprenticeships, learning to be effective at negotiating in specific contexts by doing it. They also devoted themselves single-mindedly to the study of the art and science of negotiating. This chapter will show you how to set up your own negotiation fitness program.

Key concepts will be illustrated by charting the experience of Paul, our aspiring sales executive, as he moves through multiple leadership transitions. By focusing on the experience of a single protagonist—as he deals with bosses, direct reports, customers, and other key stakeholders—you will see how the pieces fit together to provide a powerful toolbox for accelerating transitions. After all, your effectiveness in negotiating these challenges may determine whether you succeed or fail in your own new leadership role.

1

Understand Terms and Conditions

Y OU CAN'T HOPE TO negotiate your way to success in your new role if you don't understand that you will encounter many different types of negotiations. The most common mistake I see ineffective negotiators make is to adopt one-size-fits-all approaches. Unaware that there are many different types of negotiations, they doggedly apply the same strategies regardless of the situations they confront. In doing this, they exemplify the old adage "To a person with a hammer, everything looks like a nail."

Being a negotiation nail pounder is an understandable, but very dangerous mistake to make. Too often, leaders fall into this trap because they learn their early lessons about negotiation in a particular context—for example, in sales, or supplier management, or business development. Over time, and through trial and error, they develop a negotiating style that works reasonably well in that specific context. Oblivious to the reality that what works in one type of negotiation can be disastrously counterproductive in others, they keep on pounding away with their hammer rather than recognizing that a screwdriver or a wrench would be a better choice of tool.

The implication is that you, as a leader entering a new role characterized by many distinct types of negotiations, must carefully analyze each one you face, discern its essential features, and craft your strategy accordingly. There are no good one-size-fits-all approaches to negotiating; what works well in some situations will not work in others.

To become a more flexible negotiator, you must therefore understand how to identify and analyze different types of negotiations. This chapter provides some of the analytical tools you need to do this. Key techniques are illustrated through a discussion of the challenges Paul faced as he negotiated with his potential employers, Alpha, Beta, and Gamma, before signing on with one of them. You should begin to apply them to every negotiation you face, professional and personal, until they become "habits of mind."

Analyzing Negotiation Structure

The point of departure for learning to analyze negotiations is the crucial distinction between *structure* and *process*. This is akin to the difference between anatomy and physiology in medicine. One way to study the human body is to look at the major structural elements: bones and organs. Another is to looks at the dynamic processes that make life possible: respiration, circulation, and digestion. Just as anatomy and physiology are complementary views in understanding the human body, so too are structural analysis and process analysis complementary ways to analyze negotiations.

To examine the structure of a particular negotiation, you

should focus on the following six elements.[1] Together they define the "anatomy" of negotiations, from the simplest two-party bargaining scenario to the most complex situations imaginable:

- **Parties and issues.** Who is participating and what are they negotiating about?

- **Alternatives and action-forcing events.** How do the parties see their choices and what is it that impels them to make decisions?

- **Interests and trade-offs.** What do the negotiators care about and what trades might they be willing to make?

- **Information and uncertainty.** Who knows what and what are the implications for bargaining power and strategy?

- **Positions and packages.** Who is making what demands and why?

- **Value creation and capture.** How much potential is there to create joint value and to capture a share of that value?

Parties and Issues

Begin your analysis by identifying the parties and the issues. Negotiations always involve two or more parties that are exploring the potential to reach agreement on some agenda of issues. The parties could be individuals or they could be organizations. Paul, for example, is negotiating potential compensation packages (the issues) with representatives of Alpha, Beta, and Gamma (the parties).

The number of parties can range from two to dozens. If

more than two parties are involved, then *coalitions* may play a significant role in determining what happens. The issue agenda likewise can range from a single issue to the dozens of issues that are dealt with in major business deals, such as mergers and acquisitions.

In the simplest possible negotiation, two parties negotiate over a single issue. In the most complex negotiations—for example, over international trade agreements—hundreds of parties negotiate over hundreds of issues. As complexity increases, negotiators can gain strategic advantage simply by being better at recognizing it and organizing to deal with it.

When organizations negotiate, usually multiple actors *within* each side influence the negotiations *between* the sides. You need to identify who they are and figure out how they will make decisions. The decision of whether to hire Paul will of course involve his potential boss in each of the companies, but also other key stakeholders.

To analyze the parties to a negotiation, you should create a *party map* like the one for Paul's negotiation situation, shown in figure 1-1. The goal is not just to identify the potentially influential parties, but also to begin to discern how their objectives and interests differ. The circles indicate individuals, and the triangles indicate that multiple players will be involved in internal decision making within their respective organizations. One immediate implication that flows from Paul's assessment is that he needs more insight into how hiring decisions will be made within each of his prospective employers. Internal decision making within organizations often involves players pursuing surprisingly divergent objectives. The more deeply Paul understands these interests, the better able he will be to negotiate effectively over goals, resources, and the terms of his employment.

FIGURE 1-1

Mapping the parties

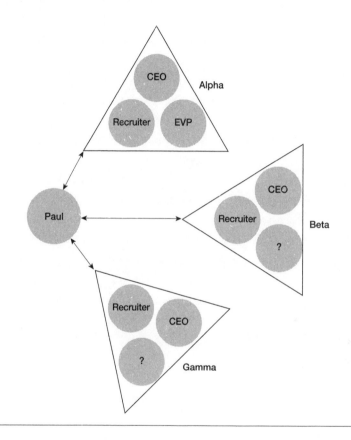

Alternatives and Action-Forcing Events

Next, focus on how the various parties perceive their choices. Everyone negotiates in the shadow of their *alternatives to agreement*, which could range from simply walking away and not doing a deal, to negotiating with someone else, to playing wait-and-see, to launching a lawsuit.[2] The stronger your alternatives, the more bargaining power you have, and the less you need to do a particular deal. One immediate implication is that you should never lose sight of your alternatives and always seek to improve them. A second is that you should look at the situation from the point of view of your counterparts. How do they perceive their alternatives? What might they do to strengthen them?

At any point, negotiators like Paul face the basic set of choices illustrated in figure 1-2. Do you accept the terms that are currently on offer, do you make a new offer, do you wait to see whether you can elicit better terms, or do you walk away with no intent of continuing the negotiations? Should Paul accept the compensation package on offer from Gamma or see whether he can elicit a better offer from Alpha or Beta? In doing so, what is the risk that Gamma will withdraw its offer?

Note that the people negotiating with Paul face similar choices. The Alpha recruiter may be trying to figure out whether to make an offer to Paul, offer the job to another candidate to see whether they take it and keep Paul on hold or break off negotiations with him.

FIGURE 1-2

Typical choices for negotiators

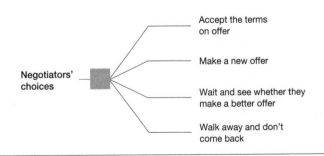

Agreement happens when both parties decide to choose "accept" over "walk away" or "wait." But at any point, the easiest choice often is to wait and see. So what is it that actually brings negotiations to closure? *Transaction costs* and *opportunity costs* can play a big role. It is costly for Paul to continue negotiating, both in terms of the work that he needs to do to prepare for and participate in discussions and in terms of the compensation he may be foregoing by delaying commitment.

Action-forcing events can also shape perceptions of alternatives and so spur negotiators to make hard choices. They are the break points that eliminate the wait-and-see option and force negotiators to make a definitive move—do a deal or walk away. Action-forcing events can be mutually agreed deadlines. They also can be unilaterally initiated by one of the parties. The recruiter at Alpha could, for example, make Paul an "exploding offer," giving him a couple of days to decide whether to accept a package before it is withdrawn, with the implicit threat that it will not be reinstated.

Contextual realities, such as the timing of planning and decision-making cycles within companies, also could act as action-forcing events in Paul's situation. At a more micro level, the simple act of scheduling a meeting or call can help move things forward. Used judiciously, action-forcing events are essential tools shaping perceptions of alternatives in negotiations. They can impel counterparts (and sometimes even colleagues!) to realize that the time has come to stand up and be counted.

Interests and Trade-offs

Once you are armed with insight into the parties and their alternatives, the next step is to focus on interests and trade-offs. Paul is negotiating over a specific set of issues, but what he is really trying to do is advance his *interests*. Interests are what you care about, the goals that you are trying to achieve through negotiation. For example, Paul may be seeking a more attractive compensation package (the issue), but he might be doing so because he wants to (1) support a particular lifestyle in the short run and/or (2) better ensure his financial security for the long run (his interests).

While negotiations sometimes involve a single issue, such as price the price of a car or the salary for a job, more often multiple issues are on the table. If so, then everyone can potentially benefit through *cross-issue trades*. To identify promising trades, you must understand interests, both your own and your counterparts'.

As Paul negotiates compensation packages with his potential employers, for example, salary is certain to be an issue. But starting date, bonus, vacation, and other benefits are likely to be important too. To negotiate effectively, Paul must define the *trade-offs* he is willing to make among these issues. What is an extra week of vacation worth to him in terms of salary? How much fixed salary would he be willing to give up to secure the upside potential of a package that more heavily weights performance-based compensation?

If Paul doesn't understand the relative weights he assigns to the various issues and outcomes, he can't negotiate effectively. Why? Because Alpha may have different trade-offs among the issues. That's a good thing, because there may be complementary needs that create the potential for mutually beneficial trades. Alpha may be happy to give more performance-based compensation to keep its fixed costs lower. But if Paul doesn't understand what his interests are, he won't be able to recognize good potential trades, and so he may leave a lot of potential value on the table.

At the same time, Paul should, following the advice of William Ury in *Getting Past No,* "step to the other side" and think about how his counterparts perceive their interests and what trade-offs they might be willing to make.[3] This is important because it can help you identify potential *complementarities*—concessions that are relatively easy for you to make but valuable for your counterparts, and vice versa.

The issue-interest grid illustrated in figure 1-3 is a tool for summarizing assessments of interests—yours and your counterparts'. The parties involved in the negotiation are the rows, and the issues are the columns. The up-down orientation of the arrows indicates the direction of the parties' preference on a given issue. Do they want more (up) or less (down) on a given issue? The number of arrows indicates the relative strength of their desires.

What does this grid tell us about the negotiation between Paul and Alpha? On the face of it, their interests are in conflict. Paul wants more salary, bonus, and vacation, as well as some time before he starts, and Alpha wants the opposite. But that ignores the relative weighting the sides assign to the issues. Alpha's desire to keep salary down is greater than its desire to

FIGURE 1-3

Issue-interest grid

		Issues			
		Salary	Bonus	Vacation	Start date
Parties	Paul	↑↑↑	↑↑↑↑	↑	↑↑
	Alpha	↓↓↓↓	↓↓↓	?	?

limit bonus compensation, while Paul places greater weight on bonus than on salary. If he and Alpha figure this out, it could set the stage for a mutually beneficial trade—a bigger potential bonus in return for accepting a lower base salary.

The question marks also tell us that Paul has some learning to do. He doesn't yet understand how much weight Alpha places on limiting vacation time or getting him in the position quickly. So this assessment also will help him identify key learning priorities. To the extent that he can do so at a reasonable cost, Paul should try to learn more about Alpha's preferences on those issues.

Finally, if you find yourself negotiating on behalf of an organization, don't forget to extend your analysis of interests to include those of the influential internal parties. One big risk you face in representing an organization is that internal differences in interests don't get acknowledged and worked through into an agreed set of trade-offs for your side. The result? You will be hobbled by lowest-common-denominator mandates that will severely constrain your ability to create and capture value in negotiations with your external counterparts.

Information and Uncertainty

Armed with insight into alternatives and interests, you can turn your attention to information. Who knows what? What would it be more valuable to learn? Like all negotiators, Paul is operating under conditions of uncertainty; he doesn't have all the information that he would like to have about his negotiation counterparts, especially about their bottom lines and interests, as well as the status of their other negotiations. This means that he has to try to figure these things out through focused efforts to learn, both away from the table and through direct interactions with his counterparts.

The old adage "Information is power" is certainly true in negotiations. In fact, good alternatives and superior information usually are the important sources of bargaining power. To illustrate why this is the case, suppose that Paul could wave a magic wand and have full information about the interests and bottom lines of his counterparts at the three companies, while they were completely in the dark about his.

This would alter the situation in Paul's favor in two critical ways. First, he would be able to make good decisions about whether and with whom to negotiate, because he would know whether there were potential zones of agreements. Second, he would be able to tightly calibrate his offers and concessions, because he would know how much his counterparts had to give. If he were armed with this overwhelming informational advantage, we would expect him to be able to get deals close to his counterparts' bottom lines.

Contrast this situation with the (unlikely) one in which Paul and his counterparts *all* have full information about each other's interests and bottom lines. What would we expect the negotiation process to look like in such circumstances? First, it would be obvious whether or not deals were possible. So the parties would come to quick conclusions about whether or not to proceed with negotiations.

Second, the negotiation process would be very different than if the parties each were highly uncertain about each other's needs and wants. We would not expect them to spend a lot of time bargaining in the usual way by exchanging offers and counteroffers. Instead, they would focus on (1) enlarging the pie to the greatest extent by making mutually beneficial trades and (2) dividing the pie through a process of *fair division*—talking about what is "fair" and very likely ending up splitting the difference between their respective bottom lines.

The upshot is that information has value, or, more precisely, having better information about your counterparts than they have about you has value. Because you are operating with less uncertainly than your counterparts, you have more control over the process. The implication is that the ability to learn more efficiently and effectively than your counterparts is itself a source of advantage in negotiations. Robert Aiello, an accomplished mergers and acquisitions specialist, has termed this "taking and holding the information high-ground."[4]

Positions and Packages

The next step is to focus on the *positions* the parties have or could take. In their seminal book *Getting to Yes,* Roger Fisher, William Ury, and Bruce Patton admonish negotiators to "focus on interests, not positions." This is often, but not always, good advice.

To see why, you must first understand what positions are and how they differ from interests. A negotiator's *position* is his or her currently stated demands on all or part of the agenda of issues under discussion. In Paul's negotiations with Alpha, his position could be that he can't accept less than $X in fixed compensation plus a potential of $Y in bonus.

Fisher, Ury, and Patton rightly worried that negotiators can fall in love with their positions and lose sight of the connection to their interests. If Paul hews too hard to his position, he may fail to see that his interests would be better served by going with a different formula for total compensation. More generally, plenty of sobering research has been done about the bad things that happen when negotiators become overcommitted to untenable positions.[5]

To help Paul avoid this trap, the authors of *Getting to Yes* would rightly counsel him to explore the interests of the other side, think hard about his own, and see whether there are creative ways to make trades and achieve joint gains. But this is not the final word on the question of whether it is best to focus on positions versus interests. Why? Because while "focus on interests, not positions" is a good rule of thumb in many situations, it definitely is not the best advice in some.

Suppose, for example, that you are negotiating in the context of a bitter dispute—trying to settle a lawsuit with a supplier, for example. Your side and the other side not only don't trust one another, they have strong mutual animus, perhaps because a history of grievances and mutually damaging acts has irreversibly soured the relationship.

Does this mean that you can't negotiate mutually beneficial deals? Fortunately, no. Bitter rivals often find ways to cooperate in the absence of trust. But agreements between bitter adversaries rarely are reached through a thoughtful discussion and integration of their interests. In fact, the simple act of trying to do so can fan the flames: "Tell me why you hate me . . ." Instead, the combatants find positions that they both can live with. In this and other cases, the best advice is to "focus on positions, not interests."

Negotiating positions often are embodied in the form of *packages,* combined sets of terms on the various issues. In the case of Paul's negotiation, these packages define the total "value" he wants the companies to offer in return for getting his services. While it sometimes makes sense to negotiate issue by issue, locking in agreements as you proceed, this is the exception and not the rule. Usually, it is more productive to table packages, because it allows you to signal the trades you are willing to make. It also helps you learn, through the reactions of your counterparts to alternative packages, about the trades they might be willing to accept.

Value Creation and Value Capture

The final step in diagnosing the structure of negotiation is to assess the potential for *creating value* and *capturing value*. This is important because negotiators too often focus on the value-capture side and lose sight of the potential to create value. When you hear the word *negotiation,* what jumps to mind? For many people, the word *negotiation* evokes an image of haggling in a marketplace or buying a car.

These mental pictures often are accompanied by a feeling that "I really don't like negotiating." In fact, for every person who relishes the cut-and-thrust of hard bargaining, there are many more who feel that they are destined to be ripped off, or simply don't enjoy dealing with a persistent haggler armed with more experience and information.

Fortunately, haggling situations are just one type, and not the most common type, of negotiation. To be more precise, they are "zero-sum" or "fixed-pie" situations, where every dollar your counterpart gains is a dollar you lose, and vice versa. They also are sometimes labeled "win-lose" negotiations, but this is a misleading and unhelpful term. Why? Because if there is a zone of agreement—that is, if the buyer is willing to pay more than the seller's bottom line, and vice versa—then both are better off reaching an agreement than not. Both "win"; the question is, Who wins more?

If you are truly in a fixed-pie negotiation, then the right thing to do is to focus on capturing the most value possible for your side. In a negotiation over a used car, this means paying the minimum possible as the buyer or securing the maximum possible as the seller. In the rare negotiating situations where ongoing relationships play no role, efforts to capture value can be pursued in their unvarnished purity, with bluffs, puffery, threats to withdraw, and all the other tools of the accomplished haggler.

Fortunately for those who hate to haggle, fixed-pie negotiations are the exception and not the rule. For most people, and all managers entering new roles, the key negotiations take place in the context of ongoing relationships. So you have to think about sustainability, and this has, as we will discuss later, profound implications for how you should best approach the negotiating process.

In addition, most business negotiations are not fixed-pie games. This is certainly the case for Paul's compensation negotiations and probably for all the subsequent negotiations he will undertake in his new role. They involve multiple issues and parties with different, often complementary interests. This means that you usually can identify opportunities for mutually beneficial trades that create value. Equivalently, you can identify ways to make you and your counterparts better off. For many people, participating in this type of negotiation—creating value and claiming value in the context of ongoing relationships—is something they enjoy doing.

The potential to create value in negotiations does not mean, of course, that goodness and niceness will prevail in the world, lambs will lie down with lions, and so on. Because even if there are opportunities to "expand the pie," the resulting value still must be divided among the parties. And to make things even more complicated and interesting, the processes of creating value and capturing value often proceed in parallel.[6] So by all means, invent options for mutual gain. But take care that you don't give away the store in the process.

Just as it is not useful to describe fixed-pie negotiations as win-lose, neither is it helpful to describe negotiations where there are rich opportunities to expand the pie as "win-win." Why? Because if by win-win you mean that the parties are better off doing a deal than they would be by pursuing other alternatives, this is true of all negotiations where there is a zone of agreement, even the purest fixed-pie haggling scenarios. And if by win-win you mean the parties walk away completely happy because they got everything they wanted, this never happens, even in negotiations where effective trading creates a much bigger "pie" of value. Division happens; it can't be avoided.

In summary, forget about win-lose versus win-win negotiations, and concentrate on creating value to the maximum degree possible while being sure that you capture an appropriate share and while preserving relationships and your reputation. Remember, if you keep the north-star goals ever in mind, you won't go far wrong.

Diagnosing Negotiation Process

With a framework for analyzing the structure of negotiations as a foundation, we can shift our focus to understanding how negotiation processes are constructed and evolve over time. The key in doing this is to train yourself periodically to step back and ask the following questions about the dynamics of the negotiations in which you are participating:

- **Frameworks and details.** What overarching phase of activity are the negotiations presently in?

- **Small steps and big bangs.** Are the negotiators pursuing narrow, incremental agreements or broad, comprehensive ones?

- **Learning and influencing.** How are the parties trying to learn from and influence their counterparts?

- **Adding and eliminating.** Are the parties trying to expand or contract who is involved and what the agenda is?

- **Bundling and unbundling.** Are the negotiators trying to combine issues or pull them apart?

- **Sequencing and synchronizing.** Are the parties trying to do things in series or in parallel?

Once again, we will use Paul's negotiations with his potential employers to illustrate key concepts.

Frameworks and Details

As illustrated in figure 1-4, negotiations tend to evolve through distinct phases, beginning with early explorations of whether to negotiate and ending in agreement or breakdown.[7] During the *exploratory phase,* the parties assess the extent of the potential gains to be realized through negotiating, evaluate their alternatives, and decide whether or not to "go to the table." This is what Paul did when he undertook his initial research, identified three promising employers, and initiated discussions with them.

Once the parties have decided to negotiate, the process shifts to the *architectural phase,* in which the basic parameters of the process are established. This phase typically includes discussions of who will participate in face-to-face negotiations, what issues will (and will not) be on the agenda, and what "the rules of the game" will be—for example, concerning the location and timing for conducting the talks. Paul's early discussions with Alpha, Beta, and Gamma, for example, established the dimensions along which he would negotiate employment packages with his counterparts.

With the architecture established, the process enters the *framework phase,* in which the parties scope out the basic formula for agreement. They do this by defining, in macro terms, the major trades across the issues they will make to create value. For Paul, this phase established that potential compensation packages would weight bonus more heavily than base salaries. Negotiators also may seek to establish guiding principles for what would constitute acceptable and nonacceptable agreements during this phase.

If the parties agree on a promising framework for agreement, the process moves on to the *detail phase.* Here the focus shifts to the tabling of specific offers and counteroffers. The parties may

FIGURE 1-4

Phases of negotiating activity

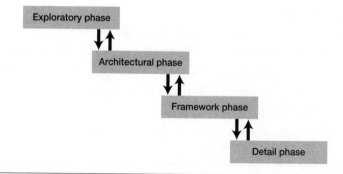

work out the details one issue at a time or through packages covering multiple issues, thrashing out the details through this cut-and-thrust. In the process, they "divide the pie" that they created in the framework phase.

These four phases do a good job of characterizing the overall evolution of negotiation through time. But this is emphatically not to say that there is an inexorable linear progression through them. If the parties reach an impasse in the detail phase of negotiations, for example, they often cycle back to search for a better formula, or even renegotiate the process architecture. In fact, skilled negotiators shift their focus quite fluidly among architecture, frameworks, and details. So if you are not making satisfactory progress through the exchange of positions, consider shifting the process into reverse gear. Move the focus back to the framework, renegotiating if necessary. If this doesn't work, step back further and renegotiate the process architecture. Then, as you get some traction, shift the process back into forward gear.

Small Steps and Big Bangs

Regardless of what phase the negotiations are in, it often is useful to assess how ambitious the parties are being in terms of their aspirations. Are they seeking modest, incremental gains or striving for more ambitious, comprehensive deals?

Extent of ambition is important because it defines the risk-reward profile for a given negotiation. Incremental gains are of course easier to achieve. Success in concluding a set of negotiations where you and your counterparts have modest ambitions also can help you build trust and lay the foundation for more ambitious agreements later on. It's hard to generate momentum if you are trying to push a very big rock uphill. For Paul, this means that it could make sense, for example, for him to accept more modest compensation for the first year if it lays the groundwork for substantial increases in following years.

But Paul must be careful. His bargaining power will decline rapidly after he has accepted the job and let go of his other alternatives. What happens if the understandings he thought were in place are not fully honored after a year? What would his alternatives look like then?

For this reason, it may be better for Paul to shoot right away for a broader, more comprehensive agreement. He should consider, for example, negotiating detailed understandings about compensation for each of the first three years, perhaps foregoing some early gains for more upside potential later on. This is a gamble, of course. But if he is confident and has been diligent in evaluating the companies' prospects, it could pay off handsomely.

There also are times when you simply can't proceed incrementally. "It does not work," the proverb goes, "to leap a twenty-foot chasm in two ten-foot jumps." Suppose, for example, you are negotiating with an organization where a few people inside are strongly opposed to doing a deal with you. They may not be able to prevent a deal from being done, but they may push for it to be a modest one and then work to complicate implementation in ways that poison the potential to do more. If you conclude this is the case, then it doesn't make sense to proceed incrementally, because it won't build confidence or create momentum. Better to shoot for a comprehensive deal that forces the other side to deal with its internal opposition, and let the cards fall where they may. If your counterparts can't confront their own demons now, there is no reason to think they will be able to do so later.

Learning and Influencing

Next, focus on how negotiators are striving to learn about and influence each other. When they are uncertain about each other's interests and bottom lines—which is essentially always the case—the positions negotiators exchange are really just "signals" about what they are willing to accept and not accept. The sides are each trying to "learn" from their counterpart's positions and the rationales they offer to support them, and to "influence" the other side by taking positions and establishing rationales of their own.

The problem, of course, is that each side's efforts to influence come into conflict with the other's efforts to learn. This is what makes negotiating under conditions of uncertainty so interesting and frustrating. Think of it as learning under adversity.

To illustrate the challenges of learning and influencing, let's return to Paul's negotiations with Alpha. Recall that a job with Alpha is his preferred choice, assuming the company meets the minimum compensation goals to which he has committed himself. Let's also assume that Paul and the Alpha recruiter have fully scoped out the agenda and identified trades that could create value. With this as a base, they started exchanging offers in the detailed bargaining phase.

But to his surprise, Alpha's initial offer came in far below Paul's minimum, in terms of both fixed compensation and bonus. The Alpha recruiter responded to Paul's expression of surprise by offering a supporting rationale that he was "untried in the lead sales role, and so we are taking a chance on developing you. If you prove yourself in the first year," she said, "you can expect a significant jump in your base compensation." When he asked about the low bonus percentage, she told him, "The reality is that your first-year results will be more a reflection of the strong base your predecessor (who was promoted to lead sales in the company's largest division) established than what you will do."

What has Paul learned and what should he do? He needs to figure out whether there simply isn't a zone of agreement here, in which case he should cut his losses and focus on Beta and Gamma, or whether this is simply an *anchoring tactic*. Research has shown that initial offers (and counteroffers) powerfully shape, or "anchor," negotiators' perceptions of each other's bottom lines. In fact, when agreements happen, they usually end up close to the midway point between the first offer and the first counteroffer.[8]

So Paul has to think hard about his next move. One option is to counteranchor by tabling an offer that is substantially above his minimum. This could level the playing field, but it could also set the stage for impasse. Even if a breakdown doesn't occur, it virtually guarantees there will be a long slog of offer and counteroffer as he and the Alpha recruiter gradually move toward middle ground.

Alternatively, Paul could try to blow the offer off the table and, even better, get the Alpha recruiter to negotiate against herself. "This is simply not in the range I'm willing to accept," he could say. "It's also way out of line with what people with my sort of experience are being offered elsewhere. So if this really is close to your maximum, then we probably don't have a basis for agreement." This is a particularly attractive option if Paul has a reasonably good offer in hand from Beta or Gamma. But even if he doesn't, it may be worth a shot.

Let's assume Paul tries this and the Alpha recruiter comes back with a more attractive offer, but one that still is significantly below Paul's minimum. What should he do now? He should look closely at the size of the concession that the Alpha recruiter made. Why? Because *patterns of concessions* often yield important insights into resistance points and bottom lines.[9] A small concession by Alpha may signal that there simply isn't a zone of agreement, while a more substantial move suggests there is still room for maneuver. In this way, Paul can seek both to learn and to influence.

Adding and Eliminating

The next step is to examine how the structure of negotiations gets established and altered. The most fundamental elements of negotiation structure are parties and issues. Once the "who" (parties) and the "what" (issues) are established, there is limited scope to influence the other key elements: alternatives, interests, trade-offs, and opportunities to create and capture value.

Skilled negotiators therefore think early and hard about who they want to negotiate with and what they want to negotiate about. It's much easier to avoid problematic partners at the outset than to try to sideline them later on. To the greatest extent possible, you should seek negotiating partners who share your "north-star" mind-set—to create value to the maximum extent possible and to capture value while sustaining relationships and reputation. This means striving to deal with "good" parties and working—within the limits of practicality, of course—to eliminate "bad" parties from the mix. Paul did this when he decided to negotiate with Alpha, Beta, and Gamma and eliminated some other potential employers from his list.

You will not, of course, always be able to deal with "good" partners. But life is too short to negotiate with jerks if there is any way to avoid it. For this reason, Paul should continue to pay close attention to how the people at Alpha, Beta, and Gamma negotiate with him, because it will offer him insight into the culture and values of these organizations and help him decide whether he wants to reside within them.

The issue agenda is likewise something that you should strive to influence from the beginning. Is it too narrow, thus offering too little potential for mutually beneficial trades? Is it so broad that complexity will swamp efforts to create and capture value? Does it include toxic issues that spoilers have intentionally included in an attempt to undermine the process? If so, then you should seek to add and/or eliminate issues.

You also should periodically step back and focus on the structure as your negotiations unfold, asking yourself, "Are the right people at the table," and "Does the agenda include the right issues?" If negotiations with the recruiter at Alpha are not going well, for example, is there any way Paul can entice other key decision makers in the company to get more involved? If there doesn't seem to be a zone of agreement, is it possible to broaden the agenda in order to create more joint value or narrow it to remove toxic issues?

Bundling and Unbundling

As you observe the process, watch how the negotiators are bundling and unbundling the issues.[10] *Unbundling* means taking an issue and breaking it down into separable pieces. To illustrate with a simple example, suppose that you and a colleague are deciding where to go for a networking dinner. Further suppose that you strongly prefer Chinese food and your colleague strongly prefers Northern Italian. On the face of it, this looks like a zero-sum situation. But before you shift into value-claiming mode, you should see whether there is potential to unbundle "dinner" into several separable issues to be negotiated. "Dinner" could consist of predinner drinks at a local pub, a main course at a restaurant, and desert someplace else. Would your colleague be willing to go for Chinese food first and then to an Italian café for desert and coffee? If so, then unbundling has opened the door for value creation.

You may likewise find it advantageous to combine, or *bundle*, negotiations that are going on separately. The larger combination of parties and issues may offer richer opportunities to make mutually beneficial trades, and so create more value to be divided. If negotiations are stalling, it likewise may be productive to split them into subnegotiations involving smaller numbers of parties and more tractable sets of issues.

Sequencing and Synchronizing

Finally, think hard about the impact of sequencing and synchronization as you analyze negotiation processes. If you are dealing with more than two parties, for example, when are you better off dealing with them one at a time and when is it better to bring them all together? If you decide to negotiate one at a time, in what order, or sequence, should you proceed?[11] Are there preexisting relationships among the other parties such that some are more influential than others? If so, should you negotiate with the more influential first or leave them for later? At what point do you shift from one-on-one meetings to group negotiations and back again?

When the agenda consists of multiple issues, you face similar sequencing-versus-synchronizing choices. When is it best to negotiate issues one by one and when is it best to table packages? If you are proceeding issue by issue, what is the most favorable order in which to negotiate them? At what point do you shift from dealing with issues sequentially to dealing with them in packages and back again?

Sequencing clearly is an important concern for Paul. He has initiated negotiations with multiple potential employers in order to test the market and gain some leverage. As he proceeds, he will have to think carefully about the order in which he engages in discussions. Should he try to generate an offer from Beta, for example, or see whether he can make more progress with Alpha first?

Concluding Comments

If you don't do a thorough assessment of negotiation structure and process, you can't hope to develop a good negotiation strategy. To deepen your understanding of the analytical techniques outlined in this chapter, pick the most important negotiation in which you are currently engaged and do a disciplined assessment of the parties, issues, interests, alternatives, action-forcing events, and the other key elements of structure. Then think about the implications for key process choices—for example, whether you should focus on frameworks or details and incremental or comprehensive agreements. This analysis provides the foundation for developing strategies that "fit" the negotiating situations that confront you, which is the subject of the next two chapters.

NEGOTIATOR'S CHECKLIST

Analyzing Negotiation Structure

What is the full set of parties that are influencing, or could influence, the negotiations? What is the full set of issues that are, or could become, the focus of negotiations?

How do the parties perceive their choices or alternatives? Are there action-forcing events that could drive the process?

How do the parties perceive their interests? What trade-offs among the issues might they be willing to make?

Who has what information? How might you gain an informational advantage?

What positions are the parties taking and why? Are the negotiations being conducted on an issue-by-issue basis or through packages?

How much potential is there to create value through trades? How will you be sure to capture a reasonable share of the value that is created?

Analyzing Negotiation Process

Are you better off trying to define a broad framework for agreement or focusing on the details?

Should you seek incremental gains or be more ambitious?

What can you do to best learn about your counterparts' interests? To shape their perceptions of their interests? To shape their perceptions of their choices?

Could you increase the potential to create value and reach agreement by adding parties or issues to the mix? Would reducing the number of parties or issues better focus the process or remove key blocks?

Would bundling or unbundling the issues help you increase the potential to make trades and create value?

Are you better off dealing with parties or issues sequentially or simultaneously? If sequentially, in what order should you proceed to build momentum?

2

Negotiate Strategically

WITH YOUR NORTH-STAR objectives in mind and a toolbox for analyzing structure and process in hand, we turn to developing some guidelines for crafting high-impact negotiation strategies. How should you approach developing the best possible strategies in the many different types of negotiations you will confront during the transition into your new role? What are the key principles— think of them as "strategic imperatives"—you should keep in mind as you work out your plans and deal with the inevitable surprises?

The place to start is to think of your new-leader negotiations as "games"—strategic interactions among intelligent "players" who are seeking to advance their interests.[1] This emphatically does not mean that we are encouraging you to engage in "game playing" in a superficial or political sense. Keep the north-star goals in mind, and you won't fall into that trap.

Instead, the game metaphor is intended to focus your attention on *how the actions of the parties are powerfully shaped by the structure of the "negotiation games" in which they are engaged*—that is, by who plays, what they are trying to accomplish, what the rules are, and so on. Equivalently, sophisticated players develop their strategies expressly to capitalize on the opportunities and to deal with the constraints that flow from different types of negotiations. You don't show up at a basketball game in a helmet and cleats.

The upshot is that negotiators must match their strategies to the structure of the negotiations in which they engage. Put another way, there is no effective one-size fits all approach to negotiating. Instead, you must carefully diagnose the negotiations you undertake and develop your strategies accordingly.

Simple and Complex Negotiations

To illustrate this core principle, let's focus on the simplest negotiation imaginable. Suppose that two people—a buyer and a seller—are negotiating over the sale of a used car. Further suppose that they don't know each other, won't interact in the future, and can't negotiate with other potential buyers and sellers. If they can't find a mutually acceptable deal, they will break off their talks and go their separate ways.

This is a "simple" negotiation because:

- Ongoing relationships don't play a role in influencing the parties' behavior.

- The negotiators have neutral attitudes toward each other and aren't enmeshed in a bitter conflict.

- The negotiation agenda consists of single issue: the price of the car.

- The bargaining range is bounded, to some degree, by the market for used cars.

- Only two parties are involved in the process.

- They are negotiating on their own behalf and not representing others.

- They are not involved in parallel sets of negotiations with other parties and so have fixed bottom lines.

You should note, in passing, just how hard we had to work to come up with a simple negotiation. Most negotiations, including all those that Paul will face as a new leader, are much more complex. This has profound implications for what it takes to be effective in negotiating in the real world.

Given the simple structure of the used car negotiation, what strategies should the buyer and seller employ? Well, for starters, there are a host of potential concerns they *don't* have to worry about:

- They don't have to worry about preserving relationships or setting precedents.

- They don't have to be concerned that a history of conflict could lead to escalation and poison the potential for agreement.

- They can't create value through trades, so they don't need to focus on trade-offs across issues.

- They don't have to anticipate and shape the coalitional dynamics that would likely arise if there were more than two parties.

- They don't have to answer to other decision makers in deciding what to offer and accept.

- They don't have to worry about synchronizing linked sets of negotiations with other parties.

The implications? Given this structure, the negotiators should focus on developing their *strategies for capturing value*. This is a classic divide-the-fixed-pie situation, and the buyer and seller should both seek to capture the biggest possible slice.

Having established this as the overarching goal, the parties can focus on developing the supporting strategies for (1) learning about the each other's bottom lines and (2) favorably influencing the other side's perceptions of what will be acceptable. To learn, they might try to figure out how anxious the other side is to conclude a transaction and do some research on the market for used cars. The buyer might also try to get information on the history of the particular vehicle. To influence each other, they might employ classic value-capture tactics such as anchoring. As the parties implement their strategies, we would predict that the process will evolve through the cut-and-thrust of offer and counteroffer, leading quite rapidly to agreement or breakdown.

Now let's compare the used car negotiation with the situation Paul is facing in his employment negotiations. To the inexperienced eye, Paul's situation could look a lot like the used car negotiation. He is presently negotiating with Alpha, and they are exchanging offers and counteroffers. So isn't it simply a matter of plowing ahead until he either gets a deal he can accept or breaks off discussions?

By now, you should recognize how very different these situations are, and have some intuition concerning the implications for strategy development. Like all leaders in transition, Paul is negotiating in the context of potential long-term relationships, so he has to be concerned about those relationships and his reputation. A number of issues are on the table, so he has to think hard about his trade-offs, seek opportunities for mutually beneficial trades, and balance his efforts to create value and capture value. He is negotiating with representatives of organizations and not individuals, so he has to be concerned about internal decision-making processes and ratification of any provisional deals he reaches with the recruiters. Finally, he has three sets of negotiations going on in parallel, so has to think hard about how to best to leverage the linkages among them. If Paul approached this situation as if he were bargaining for a used car, we would expect him to crash and burn.

Strategic Imperatives

To craft promising strategies in this and the other new-leader negotiations he will face, Paul must therefore understand the relationships among structure, strategy, process and outcomes. As illustrated in figure 2-1, different types of "negotiating games" give rise to predictable constraints and opportunities, and this has major implications for which strategies are most effective. The parties' strategies then interact to yield an evolving process as they learn and adapt to each other's moves and

FIGURE 2-1

Strategic imperatives

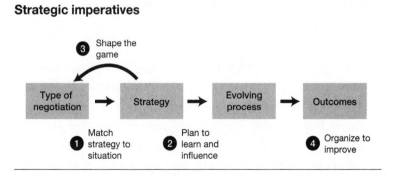

countermoves. This process eventually yields an outcome: agreement or breakdown or deferral.

Four strategic imperatives—overarching principles you should apply to develop strategies in every negotiation you face—flow directly from this model.

Imperative 1: Match Strategy to Situation

This first imperative is a restatement of the admonishment to abandon one-size-fits-all approaches to negotiating. Forget about having a consistent negotiating style. Only by undertaking a careful diagnosis of the structure of every negotiation, and by thinking through the associated constraints and opportunities, will you be able to fashion the best possible strategies. We will explore the implications of this in detail in the next chapter.

Imperative 2: Plan to Learn and Influence

Effectiveness in learning provides the foundation for your efforts in influencing counterparts' perceptions of their interests and alternatives in order to create value and capture value. Judicious prenegotiation preparation and planning is always part of an effective learning strategy. Keep in mind, though, that there are fundamental limits on what you can learn before you go to the table with your counterparts. Also, much useful insight can be garnered through dialogue with your counterparts. The implication is that you should think hard what you need to learn and whether you can best learn it through research or through at-the-table dialogue. In tandem with this learning and building upon it, you should craft positions and rationales to influence your counterparts' perceptions of their interests and alternatives.

Imperative 3: Shape the Game

By now, you should see that the metaphor of negotiations as games is a very useful one. The structure and rules of the game shape the strategy. Learning and influencing are always key parts of how you should "play."

But the game metaphor has its limitations. Why? Because there is a key difference between negotiation games and other games we commonly play. In negotiation, the players can powerfully influence the structure and rules of the game. In sports like soccer, the structure and rules are fixed. The size and shape of the playing field, the number of people on each side, the equipment, the conduct of the players, the criteria for winning, and the identity and powers of the referee all are precisely defined.

But in most negotiations, some or all of the equivalent elements of game structure are very much in play. Sophisticated players seek to "shape the game" from the moment they begin to explore the potential to negotiate—for example, by influencing who negotiates and what the agenda will be. They also seek to reshape the structure as the process evolves, both through unilateral game-changing moves and through negotiated alterations in who participates and what the agenda is.

The implication is that negotiators who are able to influence the structure of negotiations can be well on their way to achieving their goals before at-the-table discussions even begin. This reality, and the potential for achieving advantage that flows from it, is captured in the third strategic imperative: *shape the game.* This means you should think hard, not only about what the structure of the negotiation *is* and how best to proceed given the associated constraints and opportunities, but also about what the structure *could be* and how you might alter it to better allow you to create value and claim value on a sustainable basis.

As with efforts to learn and influence, your strategy for shaping the game can combine actions at the negotiating table or away from the negotiating table. You may have opportunities to "negotiate the process" with your counterparts before diving into the substance of the negotiations. You also may be able to renegotiate elements of the structure (who is participating, what the agenda is) in favorable ways as the process unfolds. At the same time, you may have opportunities to make unilateral game-changing moves—for example, by initiating other, linked negotiations—that powerfully shape your counterparts' perceptions of their interests and alternatives.

Paul was operating in "game-shaping mode" when he decided to initiate discussions with three prospective employers and not to focus on just one. He did this because he hoped to leverage his gains in one set of negotiations into gains in others. If he hadn't had the offer from Gamma in his pocket, for example, he would have been less confident in his dealings with Alpha and Beta. By negotiating with multiple partners in parallel, he influenced the structure of the negotiation in ways that helped him strengthen his alternatives and advance his interests.

At the same time, Paul made some mistakes. He decided to negotiate sequentially, beginning with Gamma. He was successful in generating an offer from the company, but it's not terribly attractive from a compensation point of view. Now he is under some pressure from Gamma to give the company an up-or-down answer soon.

He then started negotiations with Alpha and Beta in parallel. The negotiations with Beta have gone well, and he's convinced he could secure a good package from that company, but he has worries about the turnaround situation and about his potential boss. The negotiations with Alpha are less well developed, and Alpha has been low-balling him.

The good news is that Paul's sequencing strategy has left him with a bird in the hand. The bad news is that it's not a pretty bird, and he may soon have to decide whether to take it home or give it up in order to continue to pursue the opportunity with Alpha. In retrospect, he probably should have undertaken all three sets of negotiation in parallel so that they would have been better synchronized.

Imperative 4: Organize to Improve

Paul should learn from this experience and not make the same mistake again. Which brings us to the fourth and final strategic imperative: *organize to improve*. This is easy to say and very hard to do. In the midst of transitioning into a new leadership role, when you are struggling to get up the learning curve and trying to get some traction, it's all too easy to skip over this step.

But if you don't organize to improve, you have little hope of getting better at negotiating, because you won't have done the hard work to figure out what you did well and, critically, what you could do better in the future. The result? You will remain on whatever plateau of ability you have reached. This may be fine in the short run, especially if you have some natural talent. But it can become a crippling learning disability as you try to move to levels of higher responsibility. The complexity of the negotiations you confront will grow, and your skills will not.

The key, then, is to be sensible and efficient in how you approach reflecting on experience and refining your approaches. A good starting point is to discipline yourself to set aside a half hour after each significant negotiation to assess how you did in terms of achieving the four north-star objectives, by asking the following questions:

- **Creating value.** Did I do all that I reasonably could to identify and realize opportunities to create value, or did I unnecessarily leave value off the table? If the latter, why did this happen and what can I do to avoid having it happen in the future?

- **Capturing value.** Did I capture a reasonable share of the value on the table, or did I give up or take too much? If the latter, why did this happen and what can I do to avoid having it happen in the future?

- **Building relationships.** Did I preserve or enhance key relationships, or did I unnecessarily undermine them? If the latter, why did this happen and what can I do to avoid having it happen in the future?

- **Enhancing reputation.** Did my conduct enhance or diminish my reputation as a negotiator? If the latter, why did this happen and what can I do to avoid having it happen in the future?

The Negotiation Strategy Matrix

In summary, you will be better able to achieve your goals if you keep the four imperatives in mind as you develop your negotiation strategies:

1. **Match strategy to situation.** Diagnose the structure of negotiations, identify key constraints and opportunities, and craft your strategies accordingly.

2. **Plan to learn and influence.** Figure out what you need to learn and where best to learn it; use the information you gain to create value and capture value.

3. **Shape the game.** Focus on influencing who participates, the issue agenda, and the rules; don't end up playing someone else's game.

4. **Organize to improve.** Take the time to reflect on your experiences, distill key lessons learned, and disseminate them to others who are negotiating on your behalf.

These four imperatives provide broad guidelines for developing the negotiation strategies. The *negotiation strategy matrix,* shown in figure 2-2, provides a supporting tool that will help you translate the results of your situational diagnosis into concrete strategies and tactics. The matrix combines two key distinctions we have highlighted in our discussion so far. The first is between efforts to *play* the game effectively (i.e., to learn and influence your counterparts in the context of an existing negotiation structure) and efforts to *shape* the game in favorable ways (i.e., to influence the structure in terms of who negotiates,

FIGURE 2-2

The negotiation strategy matrix

Conventional view of "negotiation"

	Play the game	Shape the game
Away from the negotiating table	*Prepare and plan*—Diagnose the structure of the negotiation, and develop strategies that are a good match to the situation.	*Unilaterally alter the structure*— Proactively initiate negotiations; take unilateral actions to influence participations and linkages.
At the negotiating table	*Learn and influence*—Probe counterparts' perceptions of their interests and alternatives while seeking to influence their perceptions of yours.	*Negotiate the structure*—Negotiate and renegotiate participation, the agenda, deadlines, and other key elements.

what the agenda is, and what linkages are created). The second distinction is between actions that you take *away* from the table—before discussions begin and between rounds of talks—and actions *at* the table to enact your strategies through face-to-face dialogue.

The left-hand column of the matrix represents a conventional view of negotiation strategy: prepare and plan before negotiations and then work to learn and shape perceptions once you get to the table. Without question, it's important to do these things well, but it's not enough if you hope to become a great negotiator, because ignoring the right-hand column is like tying one hand behind your back.

You should therefore develop your negotiation strategies, as Paul has, by identifying opportunities in all four cells, using the following questions to guide your assessments:

- What information gathering and planning should I undertake before at-the-table discussions begin and between rounds of talks?

- What should I try to learn at the table and how can I best do that? How should I approach shaping my counterparts' perceptions of their interests and alternatives?

- Are there opportunities to make unilateral game-changing moves, either before the negotiations formally begin or while they are in progress?

- Can I negotiate with counterparts to favorably reshape the structure and process?

Applying the Principles

In the next four chapters, we will explore each of the four strategic imperatives in depth and apply them to develop strategies for diverse new-leader negotiations. The end of this chapter also marks the end of our discussion of Paul's job negotiations. In the real case, his negotiation with Alpha didn't go well, but he was able to secure a good offer from Beta and he took it. In the forthcoming chapters, we will shift our focus to the negotiation challenges Paul encountered as he transitioned into his new role as vice president of sales at Beta Corporation.

NEGOTIATOR'S CHECKLIST

What are the key elements of the structure of the negotiation? What are the associated challenges and opportunities?

How will you approach learning about your counterparts? What can best be learned through prenegotiation preparation, and what should you seek to learn at the table?

How will you ensure that learning at and away from the table is coordinated and integrated?

How will you approach creating value and capturing value? What mix of tactics will you employ to shape your counterparts' perceptions of their interests and alternatives?

How will you avoid becoming overcommitted to your plan and retain the ability to adapt to unexpected developments?

What is the right balance between planning and improvisation?

What personal disciplines and systems will you put in place to ensure that you reflect on experience and learn?

If negotiation ability is a key success factor for your organization, how might you approach instilling a learning ethos?

3

Match Strategy to Situation

B Y THE END of his first few weeks at Beta, Paul knew he was in for a rough ride. During the recruiting process, his new CEO admitted there were serious problems and that the company was in turnaround mode. So Paul arrived prepared to dig in.

But what he found was still a shock. The company was hemorrhaging market share, having lost three major accounts and several smaller ones in the past four months. Now Beta's largest customer, Omega Corporation, was threatening to go elsewhere. The loss of Omega, which accounted for almost 5 percent of Beta's revenue in the previous year, would be a crippling blow to the company.

As Paul learned more, he found that Beta's problems had been long in the making but came to a head with startling rapidity. His new company produced specialized industrial sterilization systems—specifically, equipment that used chemicals and ultraviolet light to disinfect surgical instruments in hospitals. The instruments in question ranged from scalpels and clamps to much more complex surgical tools such as the fiber-optic viewers and staplers used to do minimally invasive surgery. Beta's sterilization systems typically were priced at a half-million dollars and up, depending on the features. They also consumed specialized chemicals in prepackaged forms; sales of these supplies made a significant contribution to Beta's profits.

Like most medical device manufacturers, Beta had seen its margins come under pressure as hospitals, the company's traditional customers, had combined and formed larger purchasing groups. The resulting pressure on earnings had triggered some cost-cutting measures that had, in retrospect, gone too far, taking out muscle and not just fat. The company's manufacturing and quality functions were particularly hard hit when an early-retirement deal led to a larger-than-expected loss of highly skilled personnel.

Within a few months, reliability and delivery problems spiked. Fortunately, there had not been issues with the integrity of the sterilization process, at least so far, so patient health had not been put at risk. But system breakdowns forced hospitals at a number of key customers to cut back on nonemergency surgery, and the resulting drop in the utilization of costly surgical suites hit them where it hurt.

At the same time, Beta began to fall behind in delivering new systems, and this created an opening for competition. Before the troubles began, Beta had 55 percent of the market for surgical sterilization devices. The company's closest competitor had 30 percent, and had responded to Beta's troubles with aggressive price reductions and a big push to gain share. As a result, Beta had lost 7 percent of the market in the past six months, and the trend appeared to be accelerating.

Deciding that he needed to act quickly to staunch the flow, the CEO let the VP of manufacturing go. He went outside the company and hired Elizabeth, a very strong operations executive. She was tasked with addressing the issues with product quality and delivery. Now in place for two months, she had hired a number of new direct reports and appeared to moving rapidly to deal with the problems. But to date, the issues with quality and delivery persisted, leaving Beta with angry customers and vulnerable to losing still more market share.

At the same time that he shook up manufacturing, the CEO had decided, over objections from his head of sales, to make a major change in the sales force compensation system. This didn't work, and the VP of sales had quit. His departure and the problems with the compensation plan had triggered a defection of account representatives. This, of course, had further exacerbated issues with some key customers.

Paul's mandate from his new CEO is to stabilize and rebuild the sales organization, as well as assuage the anger of customers, and help reverse the loss of market share. His ability to do this will, of course, depend on how successful Elizabeth is in dealing with the quality and delivery problems on the manufacturing side. It will also depend on Paul's ability to work with his new boss.

The tipping point for Beta, and for Paul, may be the troubled relationship with Omega Corporation, a key customer. The two companies have been doing business for almost fifteen years, and really grew up together. Omega started as a small regional hospital group and grew through acquisition and aggressive building programs to become the third-largest in the country. Beta began to supply sterilization systems to Omega when it was still very small, and the CEOs of the two companies got to know each other on a social basis. Beta cemented its role as a favored supplier early on and benefited greatly from Omega's growth.

Now that relationship is severely strained. Up to this point,

Beta has enjoyed a de facto sole-source arrangement with Omega. This was based on a handshake between the two CEOs more than a decade earlier and had never been formalized. The understanding was that so long as Beta produced high-quality equipment, supported Omega's growth plans, and guaranteed "no one gets better" pricing, the company would have no need to look for another supplier. With no master agreement in place, the companies simply contracted on a deal-by-deal basis.

Now the pillars of this understanding—the quality of Beta's products and its support for Omega's growth—were very much in question. In addition to substantially higher-than-normal reliability problems with new systems in several existing hospitals, Beta's delivery problems are delaying the start-up of surgical theaters in two new Omega hospitals in the Southwest. Omega's facilities planning people are very upset, and the company's VP of procurement, Alex, is apoplectic. He was never a fan of the sole-source arrangement with Beta, believing that he could do better through competitive bidding. He and Beta's CEO have exchanged harsh words in recent weeks. He also has recommended to his CEO that Omega cancel existing contracts with Beta, go with the competitor for a major order, and bid things competitively thereafter.

This is a defining new-leader moment for Paul. If he can successfully negotiate his way through these issues and help repair the relationship with Omega, it will be a huge boost to his standing. Success would position him to carry out some major changes in the sales organization. If he can't manage these issues, Beta, and he, may end up caught in a terminal spin.

How should Paul approach these negotiations? He should start by undertaking a careful diagnosis and then *match his strategy to the situation,* our first strategic imperative. In particular, he should thoroughly assess the structure, think hard about the associated constraints and opportunities, and then fashion his negotiation strategy accordingly.

For the purpose of this chapter, we will assume that there is not much Paul can do to "shape the game." The focus will therefore be on the top-left cell of the negotiation strategy matrix, shown again in figure 3-1. With that constraint in mind, we will explore how Paul should approach creating value and capturing value in these negotiations while preserving relationships and building his reputation.

To begin to think through his strategy, Paul should diagnose his prospective negotiations with Omega along the following dimensions:

- **Relationships.** Are you negotiating a one-time transaction or a relationship?

- **Conflict.** Are you seeking to make a deal or resolve a dispute?

FIGURE 3-1

The negotiation strategy matrix

	Play the game	Shape the game
Away from the negotiating table	*Prepare and plan*—Diagnose the structure of the negotiation, and develop strategies that are a good match to the situation.	*Unilaterally alter the structure*—Proactively initiate negotiations; take unilateral actions to influence participations and linkages.
At the negotiating table	*Learn and influence*—Probe counterparts' perceptions of their interests and alternatives while seeking to influence their perceptions of yours.	*Negotiate the structure*—Negotiate and renegotiate participation, the agenda, deadlines, and other key elements.

- **Gains.** Are you dividing a fixed pie or enlarging the pie?

- **Authority.** Who has the authority to enter into agreements?

- **Coalitions.** Do the negotiations involve just two parties or more than two?

- **Linkages.** Are the negotiations linked to other negotiations?

Armed with answers to these questions, Paul can think through the implications for constraints and opportunities, and craft a promising approach for moving forward.

These six dimensions collectively represent a framework for diagnosing negotiation situations and designing strategies. Recall that our baseline "simplest possible negotiation" was the used car transaction discussed previously. The negotiations that confront new leaders are never this simple. But it's important to understand along *which* dimensions your negotiations are more complex. Moves along each dimension yield different, but predictable, challenges and implications for strategy.

Relationships: Are You Negotiating a One-Time Transaction or a Relationship?

In a pure transaction, you engage in a one-time negotiation with counterparts with whom you will have no future dealings. If you are in this type of situation, does it matter what your counterparts think about you once a deal is done? Can you do whatever is necessary to create and (especially) capture value, and not worry about sustainability or relationships?

The answer is a qualified "yes," but only if the following two additional conditions are met:

- There will be no communication, direct or indirect, between your current counterparts and anyone else with whom you negotiate in the future. If this is not the case, then your conduct could impact your reputation in ways that will make it more difficult for you to create and capture value in the future.

- The agreement you reach is "self-enforcing." That is, there is no concern that it will be abrogated or that your counterparts will fail to implement it fully. If this is not the case, then your conduct could impact the sustainability of the agreement.

Our simplest-case used car negotiation could meet these conditions if we assume that your counterpart is unlikely to be able to impact your reputation, and if we assume that the car is exchanged for cash and that's that.

But the fact that we had to work so hard to come up with a situation where relationships and reputation don't matter is telling. In fact, it's wise to assume that reputation and relationships always matter, even if you are doing a series of one-off deals with different counterparts. Negotiate with the north-star objectives in mind, and you won't go wrong in the long run, even if you might capture a bit more value in some interactions.

At the other end of the spectrum from pure transactions are relationships characterized by a high degree of trust. Though it's often used, *trust* is a word that is not very well understood. What does it mean to have a trusting relationship in a business context? What is the value of such a relationship? How are such relationships built, damaged, and restored? These questions are of considerable importance for Paul as he thinks about how to deal with the situation with Omega.

Relationships are valuable, and hence worth investing in, when they create joint gains. And three distinct sources of joint gains are bundled together in the idea of trust: *reliability, reciprocity,* and *recourse.*

Reliability is the straightforward notion that each side delivers what it promises to deliver to the other. This is valuable because it reduces the following costs for negotiators:

- **Search costs**—the costs of identifying and vetting suitable counterparts with whom to do business

- **Transactions costs**—the costs of concluding and implementing each deal; for example, the costs of negotiating and drafting contracts

- **Monitoring costs**—the costs of monitoring counterparts' actions to make sure they do what they promised to do

The result is a joint gain (actually, a joint loss that is avoided) that the parties create and divide between them. If Beta's relationship with Omega is damaged, the companies could continue to do business, but search costs and monitoring costs will increase, and the size of the "pie" of value to be divided between them will decrease.

Reciprocity is the expectation that there will be give and take between the sides *over time,* and that the ledger need not balance for each and every deal. One immediate benefit is that parties in reciprocal relationships can make *trades across time.* One side can capture more of the value in one deal with the expectation that the other side will get more in later deals. This creates additional joint value if the parties have complementary interests in terms of the timing of their needs—for example, if Omega sometimes needs Beta to respond much faster than normal in delivering systems, but can compensate by relaxing the delivery schedule for a future order.

A related implication is that the parties have what might be thought of as a "relationship bank account," with each side being able to "lend" in times of need with confidence that repayment will occur. Of course, this also creates risks. After all, people default on loan repayment all the time.

Recourse is the third potential source of relationship joint gains. Recourse means the parties have the means to enforce their agreements in the event of nonperformance by the other side. How this works depends on the extent to which the relationship is grounded in formal contracts and informal understandings. Formal contracts give the parties recourse to the courts and the law of contracts. While parties to contracts can rarely be forced to engage in "specific performance" of their terms, breach of contract renders the offending party liable to be sued for damages. The prospect of this happening, and the associated legal costs if it does, raises the expected costs of not meeting one's obligations.

If, as with Beta and Omega, a business relationship is not anchored in a contract but on informal understandings, these still can powerfully influence the parties' incentives to meet their obligations, because future gains are essentially held hostage to acceptable performance in current dealings. If Beta fails to live up to the terms of its informal understandings with Omega, the company should expect to lose the benefits of future dealings.

Relationships, in summary, are potential sources of joint gain. To the extent that you can create and capture additional value on a sustainable basis, it makes sense to invest in them. But relationships are not ends in their own right. Neither should one side be able to use relationships to capture more value than the relationship creates over time.

The relationship between Beta and Omega has created joint value, and Beta has captured a reasonable share of it. This is the reason why Paul must strive to repair the relationship, in order to preserve the relationship's joint gains. If he fails, Beta's costs of doing business with Omega will increase, the potential for making trades across time will be eliminated, and the prospects for securing future business will be reduced.

To craft his relationship-repair strategy, Paul must also recognize that the relationship between Beta and Omega actually consists of multiple relationships between people on each side at various levels. As illustrated in figure 3-2, it's useful to think of this as a "ladder of influence," with the rungs representing one-to-one relationships between people in the two organizations at different levels. The top rung is the relationship between the CEOs of the two companies. At the bottom, there

FIGURE 3-2

The ladder of influence

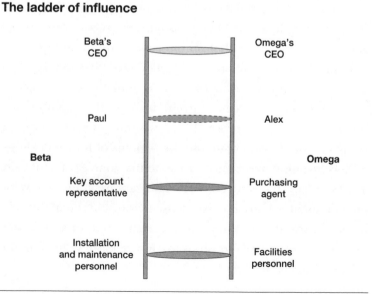

are likely to be relationships between Beta's technicians and specific users of the company's equipment in Omega hospitals. In between are relationships between Beta's account representatives and purchasing people in Omega. The dotted line is the potential relationship between Paul and Alex, Omega's VP of procurement.

Paul used the ladder-of-influence model to evaluate the state of the relationship between Beta and Omega, by making the following assessments:

- **Identify the full set of rungs.** Where are all the points of contact between the two organizations?

- **Evaluate the strength of each rung.** What is the state of the various relationships? Which are still cordial and which are strained? Which have been maintained and which have been allowed to decay? Have personnel changes on each side resulted in "broken rungs" that haven't been replaced?

- **Assess the alignment of goals and incentives on each of the "side rails."** To what degree are people at the levels on the other side aligned in terms seeing the benefits and wanting to make the relationship work? What about on your side?

Paul quickly concluded that many of the lower-level rungs in the ladder connecting Beta and Omega were still largely intact. Relationships between Beta's maintenance people and Omega staff in the hospitals had been strained, but there still was a reservoir of good will. The relationships between the key account representatives (who thankfully had not been among those who had jumped ship) and their counterparts in purchasing at Omega had likewise not reached the point of no return.

But Paul also concluded his CEO had allowed the critical "top-to-top" relationship with Omega's CEO to become dangerously frayed. The reason appeared to have been simple embarrassment, which had led Paul's boss to decide to avoid contact until he could get the problems with Beta's quality and delivery fixed. While Paul understood this, he believed it was exactly the wrong thing to do.

Then there was Paul's not-yet-existing relationship with Alex, Omega's VP of procurement. The key issue here, Paul believed, was that Alex's mind-set as a purchasing person, and his desire to make a mark for himself, predisposed him to be negative about the Beta-Omega relationship. Beta's problems appeared to have provided an opening for Alex to push for a change he long believed to have been necessary.

The implications for Paul's negotiating strategy followed directly. He had reservoirs of goodwill at many rungs of the ladder, and he needed to think about how to communicate a consistent message at multiple levels. It also helped him identify who should be on the "SWAT" team he was forming to respond to the crisis. Paul also concluded that he needed to persuade his CEO to reach out to his counterpart and communicate much more about what Beta was doing to deal with the problems. Finally, Paul knew he had to try to influence Alex, not just directly, but also by leveraging relationships at other levels of the ladder to bring Alex "back in line" in terms of doing what was best for his organization as a whole.

Conflict: Are You Seeking to Make a Deal or Resolve a Dispute?

Good relationships can create value; bad ones can destroy it. Assuming that relationships play a role in your negotiations, the

next step is to ask whether the existing state of them is contributing to value destruction and, if so, what you can do about it. The
next dimension of diagnosis, then, is to see where your negotiation situation sits on the spectrum between deal making and
dispute resolution. Deal-making negotiations are about creating and capturing value when there are neutral or positive attitudes among you and your counterparts; dispute resolution
negotiations are efforts to prevent or reduce value destruction.

It's pretty clear that the situation between Beta and Omega is
more about dispute resolution than deal making. Given that's
the case, how should Paul be thinking about the implications
for his negotiation strategy? He must understand that efforts to
resolve disputes often are stymied by two interacting factors: the
self-fulfilling nature of conflict and the existence of potent strategic and psychological barriers to resolution.[1]

Relationships have a sort of inertia. Just as it takes time to
build a positive relationship, so too does it usually require multiple bad experiences to sour one (although of course, one major
betrayal or highly damaging act can do it too). Likewise, once a
relationship has soured, it takes hard work to rebuild the basis
for trust, if it can be done at all.

This inertia is illustrated in the relationship dynamics model
in figure 3-3.[2] The key is to think of efforts to change relationships as being like trying to move a rock up and down a set of
hills. Suppose, as was the case for Beta and Omega, the starting
point is a trusting relationship, which means the rock is in the
little valley labeled point A. This is a stable state that has persisted for a long time.

Now suppose that something happens—in Paul's situation it
was Beta's reliability and delivery problems—that places a strain
on the relationship. Suppose further that it provokes an angry
reaction, leading to a counterreaction, and escalation begins.

This is akin to the rock getting pushed up the little hill to the right of point A. The hill symbolizes the fact that the relationship has some resilience to it, and so things don't immediately go completely bad. If further negative energy is not applied, the relationship will tend to settle back to point A.

But if the problems continue, eventually the relationship reaches a tipping point, shown in the diagram as point B. Beyond this point, additional contentious actions and reactions trigger a slide into serious contention, which is the point labeled C. Even at this point, there may still be some residual goodwill at some rungs of the ladder connecting the two sides. But if the pattern of contention continues, eventually the parties reach the point of no return at point D and slide all the way to a full break or a highly destructive relationship (depending on whether the combatants can disengage or not), indicated by point E.

The dynamic also can move in the opposite direction, but it

FIGURE 3-3

Relationship dynamics model

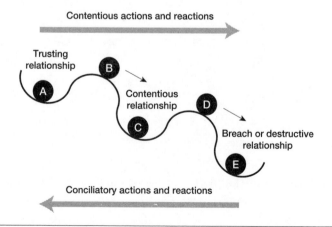

takes a lot of effort to make this happen. The relationship between Beta and Omega is somewhere between points C and D in this model. If Paul hopes to halt the slide toward a full breach and move the relationship back to point A, he will have to apply a lot of energy, in the form of effective conciliation and trust rebuilding, to push the rock back up the hill.

To be successful, Paul will have to understand and overcome some fundamental barriers to repairing relationships, represented by the hills in the model. In particular, he may have to seek ways to deal with perceptions of mutual vulnerability—the reluctance of both sides to take a chance on cooperating to create value because it leaves them vulnerable if the other side decides to focus on capturing value.

In addition, some well-documented psychological biases are likely to further complicate Paul's efforts. People enmeshed in a bitter conflict tend, for example, to view conciliatory acts by the other side as either tricks or signs of weakness. They also believe that counterparts' contentious actions are more the result of ill will than situational pressures, while believing the opposite about their own actions. This often leads to mutual attacks on integrity that further inflame the situation. In bitter conflicts, the contending parties may get to the point where they are motivated more by a desire to get payback, even if they get hurt in the process, than any rational impulse to avoid damage or create value. Fortunately, Beta and Omega haven't yet reached that point.

How does this analysis help Paul (and you) craft strategies to repair relationships that have gone bad? For one thing, it highlights the magnitude of the effort that will be required. It's going to take a lot of coordinated, consistent conciliatory action, at many levels of the ladder of influence, to turn the Beta-Omega situation around. So Paul has to prepare his own side to make the necessary investment.

Also, dispute resolution tools and techniques can help overcome these barriers. To deal with perceptions of mutual vulnerability, for example, it sometimes helps to fashion insurance policies for the other side. Suppose, for example, that Beta decided to pull out all the stops and guarantee delivery of fully functional sterilization systems to the two new Omega hospitals in a very short time frame. Suppose that Omega is worried that if Beta fails, and it hasn't contracted with the competitor, it will be in even more trouble. To reduce the risk for Omega, Beta could offer to post a substantial performance bond with a third party that would be paid in the event of nonperformance. This could both signal Beta's commitment to the relationship and greatly reduce the financial risks for Omega. This commitment also could help motivate people inside Beta to achieve higher levels of performance, and so serve as an action-forcing event.

There also are techniques that can help you overcome psychological barriers—for example, a concerted effort to act counter to expectations in order to undermine the other side's preconceptions. Key people on the Omega side—for example, Alex—may now have quite negative impressions of the Beta side. Paul needs to understand these and either directly confront them or act consistently and repeatedly in ways that clearly challenge these stereotypes. A good start would be communicating that he understands how the people on the Omega side feel, that Beta acknowledges responsibility for what has happened, and that the company is committed to making Omega whole for the costs of the failures. To the greatest extent possible, these messages should communicate the same thing, clearly and repeatedly, at all the levels of the ladder of influence connecting the two companies.

Finally, Paul should consider whether it would help to introduce a third party to the situation, perhaps someone that both the CEOs know and respect, to help mediate. Research on dispute resolution has established that mediators can help bridge gaps that the parties cannot surmount on their own by fostering communication, proposing options for mutual gains, and helping to craft face-saving solutions.[3]

Gains: Are You Dividing a Fixed Pie or Enlarging the Pie?

After Paul has assessed the importance of relationships and the current state of them, his next step is to identify the full set of issues to be negotiated between Beta and Omega. Armed with this understanding, he can assess opportunities to create value and capture value, and develop his strategy accordingly. It will be particularly important, given the state of the relationship. for him to identify and elevate potential opportunities for joint gain.

As discussed previously, if you are engaged in a single-issue negotiation, you usually should focus on capturing as much of a fixed pie of value as you can, so long as you factor in sustainability and the impact on your reputation. This means tabling offers and counteroffers as you seek both to learn about the other side's bottom line and to shape their perceptions of your bottom line.

When multiple issues are on the table, as is the case for Beta and Omega, you may be able to identify complementary interests, make mutually beneficial trades, and create joint value. In particular, you should try to identify opportunities to create value in the following ways:[4]

- **By making cross-issue trades.** If they care more about something than you do, and vice versa, then you can make a trade that creates value.

- **By making trades across time.** If you are negotiating a series of deals with the same partner over time, they may be willing to give up something later to get something now, or vice versa. If you have complementary needs, it's the basis for a value-creating trade.

- **By entering into risk-sharing agreements.** If you and your counterparts have differences in your tolerance for risk, you may once again be able to turn these differences into mutually beneficial risk-sharing agreements. If the other side is more risk averse than you are, for example, you may be able to get more of the potential upside from a deal in return for giving them more certain returns.

- **By making contingent deals.** If you and your counterparts have different assessments about future events (e.g., the price of oil in one year or who will win the World Series), you may be able to make mutually beneficial "bets."

Of course, the value that gets created must be divided between the sides. Equivalently, the processes of creating value and capturing value go on in parallel.

To illustrate this, suppose that the problems between Beta and Omega had not occurred and that they were negotiating a "normal" deal for the delivery of sterilization systems to a new hospital. The issues to be negotiated would include price, but also the features of the system, the warranty and servicing arrangements, the cost of the prepackaged supplies, the delivery and installation schedule, and so on.

Let's further assume that Beta and Omega have some complementary interests. For example, Omega may be willing to pay more for accelerated delivery than it costs Beta to achieve it. Suppose, in particular, that Omega would be willing to pay up to $50,000 if Beta could speed up delivery and installation of the system in one hospital by thirty days, and that it would only cost Beta $10,000 in overtime and other costs to do this. The net value created by this trade would be $40,000.

But how will this value be divided? Let's assume that Beta doesn't know how much the accelerated delivery is worth to Omega (or perhaps even that Omega is interested in having this happen at all), and Omega doesn't know how much it will cost Beta to speed thing up. If they share enough information, they will recognize the potential to make a mutually beneficial trade. But at the same time, they will try to capture as much of this value as they can. So the processes of creating value and capturing value go on in parallel.

The difference between these "fixed-pie" and "expand-the-pie" negotiations is illustrated in figures 3-4 and 3-5. If Beta and Omega were negotiating over a single issue, perhaps the price of a piece of equipment, then potential agreements could be represented as the black line in figure 3-4. Each point on the line represents an agreement that "divides the pie." The parties therefore seek to capture value while thinking about sustainability.

Figure 3-5 illustrates all the mutually acceptable potential deals for the full multi-issue negotiation between Beta and Omega described earlier. Potential agreements are represented by the shaded zone. In this case, it is possible to find agreements that create more or less joint value. But the value that is created must also be divided.

Of course, the two sides don't know exactly what the zone

FIGURE 3-4

Fixed-pie negotiation

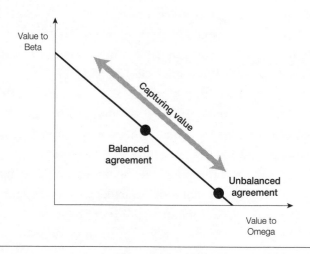

of potential agreement looks like. But if each understands the trade-offs they are willing to make, and is willing to explore the potential to make mutually beneficial trades, then they have a good shot at figuring it out. However, both also are vulnerable because they lack full information about the other side's interests and bottom lines. If they play too defensively and don't share information (or even actively try to mislead), then they may miss opportunities to expand the pie.

Any deal in the zone of potential agreement makes both parties better off than their respective bottom lines; equivalently, they all create value. But some package deals create more value than others. There are, of course, limits on the gains the two sides can achieve by exploring interests and making trades. The deals that create the most potential joint value are the ones on the curve labeled the "efficient frontier." Deals inside this fron-

FIGURE 3-5

Expand-the-pie negotiation

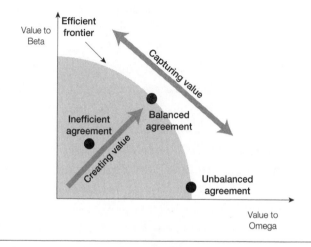

tier are inefficient in the sense that there were potential agreements, if the two sides had been able to find them, that would have made both sides better off. Equivalently, deals inside this frontier "leave value on the table."

A given deal creates value but also divides it between the two sides. Agreements around the 45-degree line are more balanced; both sides capture a significant amount of the value that is created. This would be the case, for example, if Omega agreed to pay Beta $30,000 to speed up delivery by one month. This is $20,000 more than it costs Beta, but also $20,000 less than the value that the accelerated delivery creates for Omega.

When negotiations end with agreements that the parties believe to be unbalanced in terms of value creation, it can lead to problems with sustainability, even if a lot of value is created, because one side captures the lion's share. Suppose, for example, that Omega waits until the deal is almost completely finalized and then asks for the accelerated delivery, holds the whole deal hostage, and refuses to pay more than $11,000 to get it. Beta may agree, because it recovers a bit more than the $10,000 cost, but may still feel that the deal was inequitable or the process was illegitimate.

You therefore have to balance your efforts to create value and to capture value, but this creates a fundamental strategic tension. To create value, you have to share information about your interests. But this information sharing can leave you vulnerable to being misled by the other side. The result is what David Lax and Jim Sebenius termed "the negotiator's dilemma."[5] If you share too much information, you risk having your counterparts capture all the value that you helped create. But if you act too defensively (for example, by not sharing information about interest or even actively misleading the other side), you can miss opportunities to create value.

Two simple guidelines can help you manage the negotiator's dilemma. The first is that it is generally safe to share information about the direction of your interests. For example, Omega can say, "We are interested in exploring the potential to speed up the delivery of these systems." But it is not safe to be specific about your trade-offs. Imagine Omega told Beta, "We want to speed up delivery by thirty days and are willing to pay up to $50,000 to get it." What would you expect Omega to end up paying?

The second guideline is that it is usually safest to proceed incrementally, sharing a bit of information, seeing whether the other side reciprocates, evaluating what they say for plausibility, and then deciding how to continue. By doing this, you reduce the risk that you reveal too much too soon.

While the negotiator's dilemma often is something you have to factor into your strategy, its importance depends on the type of negotiation in which you are engaged. As illustrated in figure 3-6, you can array negotiations on a spectrum from a pure fixed-pie situation (our used car negotiation) on one end to pure joint problem solving—that is, when the sides have perfectly aligned interests in seeing some problem solved or action taken—on the other. The negotiator's dilemma is not an issue at either of the poles. In fixed-pie situations, there is no reason to share information about interests, and in pure joint problem solving, there is no danger in doing so. It's the middle ground that's tricky. It's also where you find most real-world negotiations.

What are the implications of this analysis for Paul? He needs to think hard, and get his organization to think hard, about what trade-offs they are willing to make to repair the relationship with Omega. It could be, for example, that Beta could in

FIGURE 3-6

The negotiation spectrum

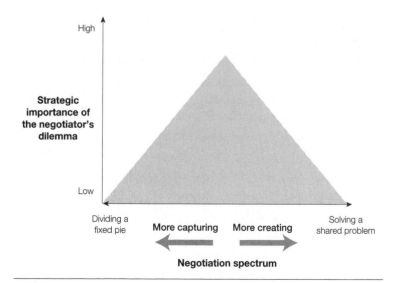

fact significantly speed up delivery of the systems Omega needs, but at a very high cost, either in terms of direct costs (such as scheduling additional shifts or overtime), or by disappointing other customers, or by taking some risks that "band-aid" fixes in the production process will hold and not result in other unforeseen problems with the systems that will make matters worse. Paul needs to figure out just how far it makes sense to go.

He should also think through *issue sequencing strategy*. Should Paul negotiate the issues one by one or in packages? It could make sense to negotiate a few easier issues first with Omega to build confidence and momentum. But he must keep in mind that it's difficult to make trades and create value if you negotiate issue by issue. So be sure to keep enough issues open to explore mutually beneficial trades. It's also usually best to avoid getting locked into agreements on an issue-by-issue basis. A good general rule of thumb is, "nothing is agreed until everything is agreed." That way, you keep the flexibility to cycle back and renegotiate terms on issues if you see opportunities to create and capture more value.

Authority: Who Has the Authority to Enter into Agreements?

Paul's next step is to assess the extent to which representatives and ratification will play a role in the negotiation process. In our simple used car sale scenario, the two parties were individuals and were assumed to be monolithic or "of one mind." So what changes when negotiations take place between organizations such as Beta and Omega?

The answer is that negotiations take place at multiple levels—within the sides as well as between them.[6] For Paul to succeed in

repairing the relationship with Omega, he of course has to negotiate with the representative of the other side—in this case, Alex,
Omega's VP of procurement. But he will also have to engage in
negotiations within his own side—with his new CEO and probably with Elizabeth, Beta's new VP of manufacturing—in order
to secure an overall agreement.

Paul should likewise anticipate that Alex will be engaged in
his own internal negotiations—with his CEO, with Omega's
facilities planning people, and potentially with other influential
constituencies—even as he interacts with Paul. So Paul must try
to understand how the other side will make decisions and who
will influence the process.

To illustrate, let's start with a simpler version of Paul's problem. Suppose, as illustrated in figure 3-7, that both Paul and
Alex are representing just their respective CEOs in the negotiations and that other internal constituencies will not play a role.
This means that they each receive negotiating instructions—or
"mandates"—that specify what they can and cannot agree to. In
order to reach agreement, the CEOs must accept—or "ratify"—

FIGURE 3-7

Decision makers and representatives

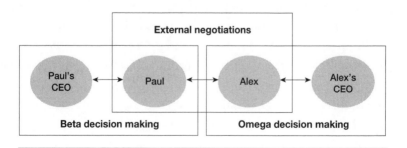

deals that have tentatively been reached between their representatives.

Tactically, this configuration could allow Paul and his CEO to play "good cop–bad cop," with Paul building the relationship with Alex and exploring potential value-creating solutions, while using the need to get deals ratified by the CEO as a way to capture value. Of course, he should expect Alex to be employing similar tactics.

But this situation also poses challenges for both decision makers (Beta's and Omega's CEOs) and their representatives (Paul and Alex). If you look at it from the point of view of Paul's CEO, for example, the challenge is how to be sure that Paul vigorously and faithfully represents his interests in the negotiations: the classic *principal-agent problem*.[7] Because Paul's interests may be different from his CEO's, and because Paul has access to information, by virtue of being at the negotiating table, that his CEO doesn't, there is the risk that Paul will not act as a faithful agent. To mitigate these risks, Paul's CEO should seek to align Paul's incentives with his own. If Paul's bonus is based on the performance of the organization as a whole, the alignment is probably quite good. But if Paul is rewarded on the basis of sales revenue on a quarter-by-quarter basis, incentives may diverge in dangerous ways. It is, of course, not possible to perfectly align the interests of principals and agents, and so the CEO also would be wise to judiciously invest his time in monitoring Paul's performance.

When the situation is viewed from Paul's perspective, he also confronts some challenges in representing Beta effectively. Because he is interacting with the other side, he is likely to see possibilities for creating value that his CEO does not. He may also become aware of external realities that people inside his organization either don't see or are in denial about. Should he try to advance the "best interests" or the stated interests of his CEO?

If Paul is able to shape the perceptions of his own side about how value can be created and captured, how does that affect his ability to be effective as a representative? It's a double-edged sword, because the more influential the other side thinks he is in Beta's internal decision-making process, the more they will try to influence this process through him. But if he is perceived as unable to influence internally, he retains the ability to use ratification tactics to capture value, but may come to be seen as a mere messenger.

Then there is the question of what Paul should do if he concludes that Alex is not acting as a "good" agent for his own CEO. As discussed previously, Alex's interests may diverge from his CEO's; he could even believe that ending the relationship with Beta is in the best interests of Omega. By putting him in charge of the negotiations, Omega's CEO has therefore created a principal-agent problem of his own, one that could result in no agreement when a mutually beneficial repair of the relationship was possible.

Fortunately, Paul has some ability to constrain Alex's ambitions. But to do so, he has to be exquisitely careful about what he communicates, probably placing more emphasis on carefully crafting a written position that reduces the scope for Alex to "spin" the situation. He also has to seek opportunities to encourage contacts at other levels of the ladder of influence. He could even open up a "back channel" with other constituencies inside Omega. Ultimately, he could move to elevate the negotiations to the CEO-to-CEO level and so reduce Alex's influence on the process, at the cost of reducing his own.

Now let's turn to the still more complex situation of dealing with multiple players within the sides. What happens when there are multiple influential decision makers within Beta and Omega with different views of "reality" and different incentives? This situation is illustrated in figure 3-8.

To meet this challenge, Paul must work to synchronize discussions at three distinct negotiating tables.[8] To reach agreement between Beta and Omega, he must foster agreement between the sides and within each side.[9]

One risk here is that the internal differences are not integrated, but you are saddled with a lowest-common-denominator position—something that everyone can agree on without having to surface and deal with the internal conflict. If this were the case inside Beta, Paul could end up with severe constraints on his ability to create and capture value in his negotiations with Omega.

He might even be forced to engage in active, potentially bruising coalition building within his own side. Suppose, for example, that he concludes that Beta should offer Omega equipment,

FIGURE 3-8

Multilevel negotiation

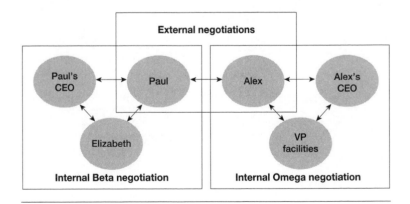

pricing, and support that will delay the working out of quality and delivery problems for other customers. Suppose further that Elizabeth has serious objections to going down this road. At what point should Paul shift from trying to build consensus internally to seeking to get the CEO to impose the "solution" he believes to be in the best interests of Beta? How does he do this without irreversibly souring his relationship with Elizabeth?

Anytime that you are overseeing negotiations among organizations, you should also ask, Who has authority to negotiate and to ratify agreements? How will decisions be made within the other side? Who influences these decisions? In the case of Omega, who has more influence—Alex or the company's VP of facilities planning? What will it take to build a critical mass of support—winning coalitions—within the other side? Within your own?

Finally, Paul has to think through the sequencing of his moves between the "outside" and the "inside." This could mean, for example, securing a broad mandate from his CEO, then engaging in early discussions externally, then returning for internal consultations—perhaps individually with his CEO and Elizabeth—so on. A related issue concerns the control of access to information: what information should he share externally? What about internally? When should he do it?

To be effective as a representative, you therefore must be like Janus, the Roman god of beginnings, who had two faces, one looking ahead and the other looking back. Your role is to act as a bridge between internal decision making and external negotiating, and to reconcile the divergent interests of fractious constituencies. This demands that you exert leadership grounded in credibility and skill rather than authority. If you participate in shaping your mandates, have a clear and unwavering vision of what you want to achieve, and work tirelessly to shape internal and external perceptions, you will maximize your ability to advance your side's interests—and your own.

Coalitions: Do the Negotiations Involve Just Two Parties or More Than Two?

To effectively shape the internal negotiations within Beta and Omega, Paul must build coalitions. As soon as you move from two-party to multiparty negotiations, the world changes dramatically because coalitions almost certainly will play a role in influencing what happens.[10] You should therefore undertake a thorough coalitional analysis and craft your strategy accordingly.

The place to begin is by asking, What are potential winning coalitions and blocking coalitions?[11] A winning coalition is a subset of the participants that collectively have the power to impose their desired outcomes on the remainder. A blocking coalition is a group that doesn't have the power to achieve their goals but can frustrate your efforts to achieve yours. It therefore is imperative to assess existing coalitional alignments and figure out whose support is critical. In the case of dealing with Omega, for example, does Alex have sufficient power to block Paul's efforts to repair the relationship by himself, or does he still have to win over his CEO to his point of view?

To influence the dynamics of multiparty negotiations, you must therefore understand who has authority and what alliances already exist. Authority is the formal, acknowledged, and accepted right of certain parties to make decisions on behalf of others. Authority arrangements can range from strict hierarchies (one person decides), to first-among-equals, to minority rules, to majority rules, all the way to full consensus (i.e., where every player has an effective veto). For Paul to be effective in negotiating with Omega (and dealing within his own side), he must obviously understand how authority functions in these organizations. Will Omega's CEO call all the shots, or is he more of a consensus builder?

Paul also should try to get insight into existing alliances, recognizing that there are different types and that this has important consequences for how he should proceed. *Shared-interest alliances* are (often) long-standing relationships between parties that have similar interests. These coalitions are inherently stable and difficult to break. *Strange-bedfellow alliances* tend to be shorter-term and more opportunistic; they are based on mutually beneficial trades of the "you scratch my back and I'll scratch yours" variety. They often are confined to a narrow set of issues and exist for relatively short durations. For this reason, strange-bedfellow alliances are more vulnerable to divide-and-conquer tactics.

To deepen his analysis, Paul should try to map influence networks within Beta and Omega and see whether he can identify patterns of deference.[12] Leaders may have authority to make decisions, but even so may defer to, or at least be influenced by, the opinions of others whom they respect.[13] If Omega's CEO really is the key decision maker on the other side, who will he or could he consult before making the decision? Who will be more influential on him, Alex or the VP of facilities planning? Does he have key advisers, whether formal or informal, internal or external, from whom he might take counsel?

Taken together, the analysis of authority, alliances, and patterns of deference will help Paul develop a *sequencing strategy*—the specific order in which you, along with other parties, can powerfully influence outcomes in multiparty negotiations.[14] Why? Because it helps you build momentum. Rather than negotiating with everyone concurrently, you can negotiate with them one at a time. This means you can try to achieve *first-mover advantage* by approaching people in a specific order that creates momentum; early success makes it easier to achieve later success.

Within Beta, for example, Paul should think about whether he should approach Elizabeth first and work out a plan with her and then take it to the CEO, or start with the CEO and secure an understanding that shapes Elizabeth's perceptions of her choices. More generally, you should think about whether you are going to use a *bandwagon strategy*—that is, starting with the easier-to-convince people and working your way toward the harder-to-convince—or a *linchpin strategy*—approaching the harder-to-convince but highly influential people early.

The choice of which way to go depends in part on what you learned through your analysis, as discussed previously, of decision-making authority. If the decision will be made through majority rules, then it may make sense to use the bandwagon approach and start with easier-to-convince people. But if the decision will be made by a single decision maker, or, on the other extreme, if everyone has a veto, then it may make sense to see whether you can convince the linchpins. If you can, then they can help you win over the others. If you can't, you haven't wasted your time getting the bandwagon rolling downhill at high speed only to see it crash into a brick wall.

As you develop your sequencing strategy, though, anticipate that other players may be trying to build or buttress their own coalitions though sequencing. Alex may develop his own sequencing plan, and it could interact with Paul's. If it does, the result could be a fierce competition for the support of pivotal people. Skilled coalition builders anticipate others' moves and get there first.

A related strategic choice that Paul may confront is not whether to deal with the other players one-on-one or concurrently, but how to use combinations of one-on-one meetings and group meetings to create momentum. In the world of international diplomacy, these two modes are known, respectively, as shuttle diplomacy and summit diplomacy. And the key is to use the right mix of both. One-on-one meetings are good for learning about other parties' positions, shaping their views by providing private information, and negotiating (potentially secret) side deals.

But the participants in a serious multiparty negotiation often will not be willing to make their final concessions unless they are sitting eyeball to eyeball. So "summit" meetings of all the parties are good settings for getting people to make final concessions and sealing agreements in public. But be careful! If the process is not ripe, group meetings can help blocking coalitions form or trigger the withdrawal of parties with veto power. In either case, you can inadvertently set up an action-forcing event that triggers a breakdown.

That said, it often is productive to move things forward by using a mix of shuttles (one-on-one meetings) and summits (group meetings). This can be combined with the tactic, discussed previously, of starting by negotiating a set of principles or a framework before proceeding to details. Specifically, you can start by focusing on negotiating a set of principles (or even the process itself), first using one-on-one meetings and then a group meeting to seal agreement. Then you can shift your focus to details and repeat the process, going back into shuttle mode and, when the time is ripe, organizing the next summit.

Finally, recall that one of the north-star objectives is sustainability. It's important to keep this in mind because while building coalitions is one thing, sustaining them is quite another. How do you ensure that allies remain on board? It is never enough simply to elicit support, because it can slip away in the night, and other players will strive to divide and conquer. You rarely will go wrong if you devote energy to buttressing and deepening your supporters' commitments.[15]

Linkages: Are the Negotiations Linked to Other Negotiations?

Finally, Paul should do a careful diagnosis of linkages among the various negotiations that will influence the overall relationship between Beta and Gamma. Recall that we began to explore issues of linkage when we discussed Paul's job offer negotiations with Alpha, Beta, and Gamma. We concluded that he had done some things well (i.e., negotiating with multiple potential employers) but might have done some things better (e.g., doing a better job of synchronizing the three sets of negotiations in time so that he wasn't forced to make commitments before he was ready).

At one end of the linkage spectrum are negotiations that are truly stand-alone, in the sense that they are not affected by other negotiations the parties have conducted; nor will they impact other negotiations that they either are conducting in parallel or will conduct in the future. In our simple used car example, the negotiations were carefully defined to be a stand-alone interaction between one seller and one buyer. The seller of the car wasn't negotiating concurrently with other potential buyers, nor was the buyer looking at other cars. So the parties' alternatives were predefined (in terms of their respective bottom lines), and linkages didn't play a role in shaping events.

But notice just how unlikely it is for any real-life used car negotiation (and any other negotiation, for that matter) to be that simple. It's much more likely that multiple linked negotiations will be going on, with the seller talking to two or more buyers, and the buyer to two or more sellers. The result is that the parties create and interact in a *linked system* of interacting negotiations.[16]

When you are dealing with linked negotiations, what changes? For one thing, linkage powerfully affects negotiators' perceptions of their alternatives. Far from being static, the seller's alternatives in his current negotiations with the potential buyer depend on what commitments he has secured (or can convince the buyer he has secured) in other sets of negotiations, and vice versa. For another, you now have to think about sequencing—in what order you will interact with other negotiators in the linked system—and information control—what information about other negotiations you will share in your current interactions. Used skillfully, sequencing and information control can profoundly enhance your ability to create and capture value in linked negotiations.

To advance your interests, you must first understand that there are distinct types of linkages, and this has implications for developing negotiation strategies:

- Two negotiations are *sequentially linked* if events in one negotiation influence events in another negotiation, but not the reverse. For example, past negotiations can establish precedents for current ones, and current ones can establish precedents for future ones. But the influence flows only in one direction, from one negotiation to another.

- Two negotiations are *interactively linked* if influence flows in both directions and events in the linked negotiations interact. The recruiting negotiations that Paul undertook with Alpha, Beta, and Gamma and the current internal and external negotiations he is managing to resolve the dispute between Beta and Omega are examples of interactively linked systems.

As the just-mentioned examples of interactively linked systems illustrate, there also are distinct subtypes of this type of linkage:

- Negotiations are *competitively linked* when one party negotiates with two or more others, but only one of the negotiations can reach fruition. When Paul negotiated in parallel with Alpha, Beta, and Gamma over potential positions, he was trying to create a competitively linked system so that he could play the potential "buyers" off against each other and thus improve his alternatives. But only one of these potential deals—in this case, the one with Beta—could get done. Of course, the companies were looking at multiple potential candidates and so playing the competitive linkage game too.

- Negotiations are *interdependently linked* when agreement must be reached in two or more negotiations in order for agreement in any of them to occur. Start-up ventures often face this sort of challenge when they negotiate to both secure funding and recruit the right people for the team. To get the people, they need the money, and to get the money, they often need the people; this is a classic bootstrapping challenge. In Paul's current situation, the internal negotiations within Beta and Omega and the external negotiations between them are interactively linked. Paul must find a way to synchronize all three "tables" to get things back on track.

To assess opportunities for advancing your interests, you should therefore ask the following questions:

- Are there opportunities to create competitive linkages that advance my interests? Can I undercut others' ability to use competitive linkage against me by cooperating with other players?

- Will the creation of interdependent linkages give me access to important resources and/or improve my bargaining position? Can I bootstrap by offering commitments of the "if I can get them to agree, will you agree" sort? Can I find ways to eliminate constraining interdependent linkages? For example, if Paul decides to initiate CEO-to-CEO discussions to resolve the Beta-Omega dispute, he is effectively collapsing the internal-external linked system into a single person-to-person negotiation.

Finally, anytime you are dealing with linked systems, the sequencing of moves among the various linked negotiations is important. Paul's position as the bridge between the external negotiation with Omega and the internal negotiations within Beta opens the opportunity for him to manage the flow of information among them. In competitively linked negotiations, you have to think about whom to approach first, how detailed an offer to try to elicit, and when and how to begin to shop that offer to others.

Concluding Comments

In the end, Paul scored a big win in repairing the relationship between Beta and Omega. He catalyzed a series of discussions with the CEO and Elizabeth, and other key internal constituencies. The conclusion was that Beta should take some risks, in terms of potentially angering other customers, to pull out the stops on the Omega account. Elizabeth had made enough progress on the quality and reliability issues to enable Beta to make some ambitious new delivery commitments for the two Omega hospitals.

Paul then persuaded his CEO to deliver the proposal in person to the head of Omega. This helped short-circuit the internal decision-making process inside Omega and reduced Alex's influence. Paul understood that Alex would be covertly furious about this and still out to transform the Beta-Omega relationship. But he counted on being able to either win over Alex as things moved forward or simply hope the relationship would outlast Alex's tenure.

The meeting between the two CEOs seemed to go well. Paul had wrung a promise from his CEO that he would open with a sincere apology for what had happened and a personal commitment not to let it happen again. This, combined with the ambitious promises and Beta's subsequent ability to meet them, put things back on a reasonably even keel. Paul was aware that a door had been opened to a very different, less close relationship between the companies. But given what had transpired, a return to near status quo was the best anyone could hope for.

Negotiator's Checklist

Relationships

Is it a one-time interaction or part of a longer-term relationship?

Even if it is the former, are there implications for other relationships and your reputation? If the latter, how does that relationship create value?

Conflict

Do you and your counterparts have neutral or positive attitudes toward each other, or are you negotiating in the context of a dispute?

What can you do to stabilize the situation and avoid additional escalation?

Can you move the situation "back up the hill," and if so, how? Is your objective relationship repair or divorce?

Gains

What is the full set of issues to be negotiated?

What are your trade-offs? The other side's?

What are the implications for how you will approach creating and capturing value?

Authority

How will "internal" negotiations interact with "external" negotiations?

If you are a representative, how should you approach clarifying roles and securing your mandate?

Parties

Who will participate in the negotiation, and what are their sources of power?

What are potential winning and blocking coalitions?

What are the implications for sequencing? For the use of shuttles and summit meetings?

Linkages

How are your current negotiations linked to other negotiations?

What are the implications for the sequence of "moves" you should make in the linked system?

What are the implications for how and when you should share information?

4

Plan to Learn
and Influence

PAUL'S SUCCESS IN DEFUSING the crisis with
Omega was a key "early win." He got a big credibility boost with his peers, his team, and his boss.
It established him as a force to reckon with in the organization
and helped reenergize the troops in the field.

But he knew he couldn't afford to rest on his laurels. Elizabeth was rapidly sorting out Beta's production and reliability
problems. Very soon, the company would be ready to launch a
broad counterattack on the competition. Sales would have to
be ready to lead the charge.

Paul had begun to put the foundations in place. Working
with Beta's VP of HR, he launched a recruiting drive to the fill
the slots vacated by the mass defection of reps and hired a new
director of sales training. He also had engaged a compensation
consultant to design a new plan for the sales force. He had
already talked with Elizabeth about setting up a cross-functional
team to coordinate sales and production, with a mandate to balance growth with quality and sustainability.

But one critical gap remained unfilled: IT support for the sales force. It was an understatement to say that the existing sales support system, CustomerContact, was antiquated; it had, so far as Paul could tell, been designed in the early Paleozoic era. The database was rickety, the functionality limited, the connections to other company systems nonexistent, and the interface awful. Unsurprisingly, only a small percentage of Beta's sales reps actually used it, beyond doing what was mandated for reporting purposes. So customer data was fragmentary and out of date. If the system had ever been live, it certainly had died a long time ago.

Paul knew what he wanted to do: purchase and implement SalesForcePlus, the state-of-the-art industry leader. It combined an easy-to-use customer database with excellent planning and reporting tools. It also would integrate seamlessly with Beta's existing enterprise resource planning system on the production and fulfillment side. Paul had used it at his previous company, and he was confident that it could dramatically reduce costs and increase sales productivity at Beta.

The problem was the required investment. A baseline implementation of SalesForcePlus would cost close to $3 million, and the additional features Paul wanted would run an additional $1 million. Paul did his homework and floated an initial proposal, backed up by a solid business case, to Beta's CEO and CFO. The CFO had immediately balked, saying that Beta couldn't afford to be making this sort of investment until the company was back on a more stable financial footing. While less negative, the CEO also had expressed concern, asking Paul whether he could "make do" with the existing system for the next year or find a less expensive solution.

Paul believed this was not the time for half measures. If Beta was going to reverse the tide and meet competition head-on, the sales force had to have the right kind of support. Doing nothing meant that opportunities would be lost and things could easily fall through the cracks in ways that would further alienate Beta's customers. But implementing the wrong system would be even more damaging. While there were other, less expensive options out there, they all had significant drawbacks. And once the company purchased a system, it would be locked in for the foreseeable future. Paul concluded he would rather wait and get the right system. If this meant struggling along with CustomerContact, so be it.

But he wasn't going to give up without making a strong effort to convince the CEO and CFO. His next big new-leader negotiating challenge, then, is figuring out how to influence these two people. His goal is to have them come to see that the short-term costs would be more than offset by the medium-term benefits, as well as by the reduction in the risk of further alienating customers at this critical time.

As discussed previously, Paul should start by diagnosing the structure and thinking through the implications for his strategy. The players include the CEO, the CFO, Elizabeth, and Ted, the VP of IT. As a result of his first few months at Beta, Paul had a pretty good sense of the influence networks at the top of the company. Using a sequencing strategy, he approached Beta's VP of IT early and found Ted eager to get a new system implemented but agnostic about what system to go with. He likewise approached Elizabeth and found her to be sympathetic. Like Paul, she didn't want to get enmeshed in a systems integration nightmare and would rather have no system than the wrong one. But she also had some concerns about the capacity of her organization to absorb the integration work.

While support from Ted and Elizabeth would help on the margin, their collective influence on the CEO and CFO was limited. So the main action in this negotiation had to happen "at the table," in discussions between Paul and the key decision makers. In terms of the negotiation strategy matrix, shown in figure 4-1, Paul must operate in the lower-left cell. He must effectively "learn and influence" in a series of face-to-face interactions.

Interests and Alternatives

You can influence people in two fundamental ways. The first is to convince them that proceeding in the way you desire is in their *interests*. The second is by having them come to see that your desired course of action is their *best alternative*.

Interest-based persuasion involves getting others to see that their own wants and needs will be served, to an adequate degree, by going down the road you propose. As discussed in the previous chapter, this includes identifying mutually beneficial trades that create joint value while dividing the pie in a way that is

FIGURE 4-1

The negotiation strategy matrix

	Play the game	Shape the game
Away from the negotiating table	*Prepare and plan*—Diagnose the structure of the negotiation, and develop strategies that are a good match to the situation.	*Unilaterally alter the structure*—Proactively initiate negotiations; take unilateral actions to influence participations and linkages.
At the negotiating table	*Learn and influence*—Probe counterparts' perceptions of their interests and alternatives while seeking to influence their perceptions of yours.	*Negotiate the structure*—Negotiate and renegotiate participation, the agenda, deadlines, and other key elements.

acceptable. Doing this, in turn, requires that both you and they understand your respective interests and the trade-offs you are willing to make.

The implication is that Paul needs to understand much more about the interests of Beta's CEO and the CFO. What do they really care about? Or, perhaps more importantly, what are they most concerned about? What trade-offs are they willing to make? What risks are they trying to avoid? What do they need and what do they want? To proceed, Paul must know much about these two people and how they are viewing the situation. Only then will he know how best to frame his arguments.

To deepen his understanding, he should assess the *driving forces and restraining forces* acting on the CEO and CFO.[1] People facing tough decisions experience opposing sets of forces pushing them in conflicting directions. Driving forces push them in the direction you want them to go, and restraining forces in other directions. The source of tension might be internal conflict (Do I want X more than Y?) or external social pressures (What about the promise I made to Z?). If the pressures are significant and opposing, the person is likely to defer commitment until confronted with an action-forcing event. The essence of interest-based persuasion, then, lies in strengthening the driving forces and weakening the restraining forces.

The second path to achieving your desired results is through *alternatives-based persuasion.* How do people perceive their alternatives? Are there things you can do to influence this—for example, by opening up new possibilities or by "pruning" the tree of viable options? This is, incidentally, a technique that parents learn early on in dealing with their children. "How much more time do you want to stay at the park?" is a dangerous question. "Do you want ten more minutes?" is much safer.

The implication is that Paul must understand much more

about how Beta's CEO and CFO perceive their alternatives in this situation. If the answer is, "Invest in this costly system, or wait and do it later with no damage done," then he has a lot of work to do. Fortunately, there is still much he can do to reshape their perceptions of alternatives.

Learning at the Table

The next step, then, is for Paul to engage in some focused learning about the interests and perceived alternatives of the CEO and CFO. In part, he can do this through conventional prenegotiation preparation—for example, by having conversations with people who know, and perhaps advise, the two executives. But this sort of preparation can only take him part of the distance he needs to travel in terms of gaining deeper understanding.

"Be prepared" is probably the most often uttered advice about negotiation. How many times have you been admonished to undertake thorough preparation—both about the substance of negotiation and about the people on the other side—before going to the table? How often have you likewise been advised to plan your moves in exquisite detail and to anticipate the countermoves and counter-countermoves far out the tree of possibilities?

So long as it is not taken too far, "be prepared" is good advice. Of course, you would not want to negotiate unprepared, if reasonable investment in research and analysis would enhance your ability to create and capture value. Neither would you want to seem to be thrashing around if a reasonable amount of effort in planning could have helped prevent it.

The key word, though, is *reasonable*, because it's simply not possible to learn all you would like to learn before negotiating, nor is it possible to create plans that anticipate all possible contingencies. There are limits and cost-benefit trade-offs in terms of preparation and planning that simply can't be ignored.

You can't learn everything you want, because much valuable information simply isn't available, regardless of how much time and energy you have to invest. Other information may potentially be available but at a cost, in terms of your time and other resources, that far exceeds its value.

In this case, there is relatively little value in Paul's guessing what the CEO and CFO care about and how they perceive their alternatives; he would do better to gather that information at the table through direct interactions with the two executives. He should therefore carefully think through both the "what"—what does he most need to learn?—and the "how"—how can he best acquire the information he needs? Put another way, what are the key actionable insights, and how can he gain them most efficiently and effectively?

Much of the "what" has already been discussed. To understand their interests, Paul should seek to gain insight into the driving and restraining forces acting on them. To paraphrase Roger Fisher, he needs to figure out whether there is a "yesable proposition," and if so, what it is.[2]

The starting point, then, is to figure out why his current proposal is eliciting a no, stronger in the case of the CFO but also emanating from the CEO. Paul already has clues about this. They are balking at the required investment (a restraining force) and don't perceive a sense of urgency or downside to waiting (lack of a driving force). But before Paul acts, he would be well advised to validate this hypothesis and dig a lot deeper to be sure that hidden forces are not playing a critical role.

At the same time, Paul must explore how the two executives perceive the alternatives. According to his previous interaction, they appear to see it as a simple yes/no, invest-or-don't-invest choice. But once again, Paul would be well advised to look deeper, to see whether there is awareness, on the part of one or both of the executives, that there is a broader range of options.

The "How" of Learning

Given that Paul will focus on learning directly from the CEO and CFO, how should he approach the learning process? He should start by dealing with the two executives separately. Why? Because, as discussed in the previous chapter, he is likely to gain more insight in private meetings, where the CEO and CFO are not acting as each other's audience. It could emerge, for example, that the CEO is less opposed than he appears and was simply influenced by the CFO's initial response. Or it could be that the CFO feels that he needs to demonstrate to the CEO that he is firmly on top of the company's finances. So additional three-way meetings are unlikely to be helpful at this time.

Paul also has to make a sequencing decision: whom should he talk to first? If Paul is certain the CFO is strongly opposed, then it may make sense to talk to the CEO first. But the risk is that this will cause the CFO to further harden his position. On balance, it probably makes sense to go with a linchpin strategy and talk to the CFO first.

Then there is the question of how Paul should approach these meetings. He should start by establishing the learning objective: "I know that you have reservations about making an investment in SalesForcePlus right now. Can we talk a bit more about them?"

Once in the meetings, Paul should focus mostly on "active listening" and avoid getting into arguments about the merits of the investment. His objective is both to learn and to be seen to be genuinely seeking more insight. Listening, simply but intensely, is itself a powerful form of persuasion. To engage in active listening, Paul should follow these guidelines:

- **Pose questions that stimulate reflective responses.** Avoid questions with yes/no answers or ones that provoke knee-jerk restatements or defensive reactions. "Why are you so opposed to a system the company needs so much?" is not a good question. "I understand that you are worried about our capacity for investment right now; can you tell me more about your concerns?" is much better. Paul should take the time to write out a few good questions before the meeting.

- **Triangulate on key issues.** Ask the same basic question in two or three ways (not all at once, of course, but over the course of the meeting) in order to see how consistent the answers are. By doing this, you often can elicit additional, hidden restraining forces. Of course, you need to be careful in doing this not to appear that you don't believe what you are hearing or aren't listening!

- **Summarize and test comprehension.** Feed back what you are hearing both to demonstrate that you have been listening and understand the other person's perspective and to test that you really have. Note that summarizing and testing comprehension rapidly bleeds over into active persuasion. So be careful you don't take it too far. No one likes having their statements twisted or caricatured.

- **Use "what-ifs" to probe the depth of opposition.** Statements of the form "If *x* were to be true, would it allay

your concerns?" can help you gain deeper insight into
the nature and depth of restraining forces. Here too,
active listening opens a door to persuasion. Done well,
it can transform a positional exchange into a dialogue
on what it would take to go down the road you desire.

- **Watch for "hot button" reactions.** As you ask questions
  and feed back what you have learned, look carefully for
  what generates strong emotional reactions, because
  this also can provide insight into restraining forces.
  Judiciously probe these reactions, perhaps by making
  leading statements such as, "You seem to feel strongly
  about that . . ." But once again, be careful not to trigger defensive reactions unnecessarily.

As you engage in active listening and seek to gain actionable
insights, take care not to fall into two common traps. The first
trap, mentioned earlier, is to inadvertently trigger defensive
reactions, causing the other party to become even more committed to their position and unwilling to explore value-creating
solutions. So watch out for defensive body language (e.g., the
crossing of arms or legs, pushing back from the table or desk),
and if you observe it, back off and give the person a chance to
recover and reengage.

The second trap is to engage in *self-fulfilling learning*. For you
to learn effectively in negotiation, your efforts must be disciplined and directed by a "point of view," hypotheses you begin
to develop early on concerning the nature of your counterparts'
interests and promising frameworks for a deal. But take care that
your prior judgments don't overly bias your information gathering and lead you astray. It's essential that you keep the distinction between assumptions and hypotheses clear in your mind.

In this case, Paul's conversations largely (and correctly) confirmed his prior hypotheses. The CFO was quite focused on minimizing short-term investment, and the CEO was sympathetic to that view. He also concluded that they didn't see the sales support system as a "burning platform" issue that would justify breaching fiscal discipline.

At the same time, though they still were largely viewing it as a yes/no decision, he had succeeded in convincing them that it was worth considering other options. His meeting with the CEO ended with agreement that Paul would do some additional analysis and come back with a broader set of potential alternatives.

Beyond doing the background research about systems and costs, what should Paul do to prepare for the next stage of the negotiations? He should think about how to influence their perceptions of their interests and their perceptions of their alternatives. This means he should be thinking hard about framing and choice-shaping strategies.

Framing (and Reframing)

Framing is about influencing the frame of reference your counterparts use to assess their interests and make trade-offs. What do they think "the problem" is, and how, therefore, do they decide what is at stake? How can you influence these perceptions? To return to the example of influencing a colleague to go for Chinese food rather than Italian, you may prefer the person to apply a "health" frame of reference to make the decision.

Framing works because people's assessments of their interests crystallize only when they are confronted with the need to make specific choices. Also the "mental models" people use to make sense of a situation depend on how that situation is presented.[3] (See "Risk and Loss Aversion.")

Risk and Loss Aversion

People tend to be both risk averse and loss averse. Risk aversion means that that people are willing to give up potential upside in return for gaining certainty. If you were offered a choice between $200,000 for certain or a fifty-fifty gamble at getting $450,000 or nothing, which would you take? For most people, the answer is the $200,000. This is risk-averse behavior, though, because the expected value of the bet is $225,000.

Loss aversion means that people are more sensitive to potential losses than potential gains. If you were forced to choose between (1) a fifty-fifty gamble at winning $200,000 or getting nothing and (2) a fifty-fifty gamble at winning $500,000 or losing $200,000, which would you take? Again, for most people the (loss-averse) answer is choice 1, even though the expected value of that choice, $100,000, is less that that of the other, $150,000.

There are straightforward implications for framing. Those who are trying to oppose some action will often try to accentuate the risks and play up the potential for losses. One way to counter this is to show that all courses of action have risks and create the potential for losses. Another is to find ways to mitigate or avoid the potential for losses.

Your mental models are the product of your formative experiences, professional training, and cultural heritage; they embody your guiding assumptions and values, your sense of what is important, your beliefs about cause and effect, and your expectations of others' behavior.[4] They provide you with rules of thumb and scripts for "making sense" of new situations.[5]

In dealing with the CFO, for example, Paul should not be surprised if financial models will play a critical role in his thinking. Paul is proposing an investment, so he needs to understand how investments are evaluated by financial professionals. Suppose, in addition, that the CFO experienced a near bankruptcy in a previous company. How might that affect the mental models that he applies to "make sense" of the current situation?

Without mental models, you would have to figure out each new situation from scratch. But reliance on mental models can promote rigidity and stifle learning. The frameworks that we use to interpret reality are so deeply embedded in our psyches that we tend to be unaware of our biases. As a result, people block out information that is inconsistent with accepted "truths"—a process known as *selective perception*. People also tend to seek evidence that confirms accepted truths.[6]

This is why it is so important to begin shaping perceptions early, before the people you want to influence decide what is at stake. At the early, formative stage of decision making, it is relatively easy to influence *which* mental models get activated. So the essence of framing is posing the problem in ways that activate the "right" mental models—ones that lead to the conclusions you believe to be the correct ones—and avoid activating the "wrong" ones. The following are examples of commonly used framing techniques:

- **Invoking the common good.** This approach involves emphasizing collective benefits and downplaying individual costs.

- **Linking to core values.** Marketers and propagandists long ago learned the power of linking choices to the values that define self-identity.

- **Heightening concerns about loss or risk.** This means loss and risk aversion biases. Desired courses of action can be cast in terms of potential gains, and undesired choices in terms of potential losses. Likewise, desired courses of action can be characterized as less risky, undesired choices as more risky.

- **Rejection and retreat.** Another technique for shaping perceptions of interests is to ask for a lot initially and then settle for less. This works because people tend to "anchor" on the initial request and view subsequent moves toward a more moderate request as concessions.[7]

- **Narrowing or broadening the focus.** Sometimes choices are best posed broadly, at other times narrowly. A choice that could be construed as setting an undesirable precedent might best be framed as a highly circumscribed, isolated situation independent of other decisions. Other choices might be better situated within the context of a higher-level set of issues.

- **Enlarging the pie.** Choices perceived as win-lose propositions are particularly difficult to sell. Broadening the range of issues under consideration can facilitate mutually beneficial trades that "enlarge the pie."[8]

- **Inoculating against expected challenges.** As far back as Aristotle, persuaders have been advised to inoculate their audiences against the arguments they expect their opponents to make. Presenting and decisively refuting weak forms of expected counterarguments immunizes audiences against the same arguments when they are advanced in more potent forms.

- **Providing a script for convincing others.** Effective framing doesn't just influence the immediate person you are trying to influence, but also provides that person with a persuasive script for convincing others.

In retrospect, then, Paul made some serious framing mistakes early on. By posing the problem the way he did, as a choice between buying an expensive, world-class system or doing nothing, he not only set himself up for a no, he probably activated the wrong mental models in the key decision makers. Now they are viewing the sales support system as "discretionary investment in times of serious resource scarcity."

Now he has to try to *reframe* the situation—shift perceptions of what is at stake and the evaluative criteria that the CEO and CFO will use to evaluate options and make a decision. Reframing is a much more difficult proposition than framing, in part because people are reluctant to change their mind once they have reached a preliminary conclusion. What shift in the frame of reference should Paul seek to have a fighting chance of getting the conclusion he believes to be the right one? Once he has figured this out, how should he approach making this shift happen?

The answer is that he wants the CEO and CFO to see a no as having serious potential consequences for the success of the turnaround effort. Right now they believe there is essentially no cost to waiting and procuring a system once the financial situation has stabilized. Paul has to directly confront the belief that "no" has no consequences. Ideally, he would be able to reframe the choice as "either we implement a proven sales force support system or we risk serious miscues in dealing with customers and in processing orders rapidly and reliably." His case might further be strengthened with a few horror stories of things falling through the cracks because of the existing system. Paul should also situate the decision in the context of the fragile state of customer relations and low morale in the sales force.

To back this up, Paul has some more data collection and analysis to do. He needs to do a better job of documenting the costs of the failures associated with the existing system. In doing this, he should look beyond the sales function and assess the impact on the production and fulfillment side of the business. Is the existing system creating problems there too? Are there potential gains in timeliness and efficiency to be realized from the opportunity to integrate SalesForcePlus with operations' resource planning system? Elizabeth should be able to help him make these assessments. At the same time, he has to do a better job of benchmarking—figuring out what competitors are using and what the benefits are as part of a broader effort to document the potential gains from implementing the system.

Then there is the question of how he should approach reframing. One of the core insights of research on persuasive communication is the power of focus and repetition.[9] Paul's arguments are likely to take root in the minds of the CEO and CFO if they consist of a few core themes, revisited many times. This does not mean, of course, using same words over and over; that makes it apparent that you are trying to persuade, which can provoke a backlash. It does mean that Paul should be prepared, if he really believes this is important, to keep coming back to make his case, probe the points of resistance, and seek to address them.

Paul also should think about the modes through which he will make his case: verbally, in writing, or a combination. Decisions about how to communicate a message should not be made lightly. Complex technical and data-intensive arguments are usually best conveyed in written form, with appropriate summaries. But the key points must usually be amplified and placed in context through (multiple) face-to-face meetings.

As you are negotiating, keep in mind that framing and position taking must go hand in hand. Think of a negotiating position as a building that has to be constructed on a firm foundation. The goal in framing is to lay that foundation down plank by plank. Any position you take should therefore backed up with a supporting rationale that conveys information about your interests, provides facts and logic to support your case, and, critically, influences how the other side thinks about their own interests. Likewise, you shouldn't make a concession without a supporting rationale. So concessions and reframing also must be closely coordinated.

Finally, keep in mind that you are not the only one who will be trying to shape perceptions of interests through framing. Your counterparts on the other side will, of course, try to do the same, and this often results in a "frame game"—a contest to see whose view of "the problem" is the most compelling. You should therefore think hard about how others are likely to use framing and preemptively inoculate the people you are trying to influence against their arguments.

Choice Shaping

Framing perceptions of interests is the hammer of persuasion; shaping perceptions of alternatives is the anvil. While critical, Paul's efforts to influence the CEO's and CFO's perceptions of their interests might not be enough, because they still see the choice as a "go/no-go" decision on a major investment at a difficult time. For this reason, Paul should marry reframing with choice shaping, with the goal of creating a broader set of alternatives for their consideration.

One approach to choice shaping that Paul should consider is *option pruning*. This means convincing people that an option they are considering is not in fact viable. Paul could make the case, for example, that it is not an option to stay with the existing system—that the problems are so serious that the question is not whether or not to buy a new system, but which system to purchase. The virtue of this approach, if it works, is that it shifts the focus to evaluation of alternative systems investment proposals. But Paul should think hard before going down this road, because this could easily be the first step toward locking the company into a cheaper alternative to SalesForcePlus, and that could be worse than no new system at all.

Unbundling is another useful approach to reshaping perceptions of choices. As it stands now, the two executives are confronted with a choice between investing $4 million in a full-scale implementation of SalesForcePlus and doing nothing. Paul might be better able to achieve his objectives if he unbundled the larger investment into a set of smaller, more digestible ones. He could, for example, unbundle the investment into three distinct pieces:

- Baseline implementation of a system for the sales force

- Integration with operations' resource planning system

- Additional planning and reporting functionality

He could then develop cases for investing in each. The result of this unbundling is that the CEO and CFO would have a "menu" from which to choose. A $3 million investment to get the first two elements could be more palatable, if presented this way, than the full $4 million implementation. The downside, of course, is that Paul might not get everything he thinks is justified. So he needs to assess the likelihood that he can hit a home run, and then decide whether he is better off settling for hitting a solid double.

Unbundling tactics can often usefully be combined with *incrementalism* to shape perceptions of choices. Paul could seek, for example, to get the baseline implementation of the system included in this year's budget, with the understanding that the integration with operations, and potentially the added functionality, will be funded next year. The virtue of this approach is that it means that Beta will be committed to SalesForcePlus. The downside, once again, is that Paul won't immediately get what he believes to be necessary to address the company's critical issues.

If the CEO and CFO still are reluctant to make the investment, Paul could try to stage the investment out even more. He could, for example, propose a pilot program to try the new system with his key-accounts group and, depending on the results, extend it to the full sales force. If he has any doubts about the system, or about his organization's ability to absorb it, this also would help him manage risk. It also has the virtue of impelling the IT group to do most of the groundwork for an organization-wide implementation. The downside, once again, is time and impact. So he needs to assess the costs and benefits of a "big bang" implementation, as opposed to a staged rollout.

Paul could try to highlight and overcome constraints. The key constraint in this case appears to be the availability of investment capital. Implicit in the CEO and CFO's reluctance to invest is the message that "if this were a normal year, this would be an investment we could look favorably on." So the problem is not really about perceptions of costs and benefits, it's about the availability, in this financial period, of capital. Armed with this insight, Paul might think about creative ways to reduce the magnitude of the required investment for this budget cycle while still getting the system he needs.

He could, for example, initiate linked negotiations with the supplier of SalesForcePlus about its payment terms. Would it be possible to enter into a contract but shift a significant portion of the cost into the next year, or otherwise stage out the payments? In fact, the constraints that Beta is facing could actually be a source of leverage for him in the negotiations with the supplier. Naturally, he would need buy-in from the CEO and CFO to go down this road.

One way he might do this is to *negotiate the process* with the key decision makers first, before proceeding on to debating the substance. One mistake Paul made was to jump directly into advocating for a specific system without first establishing *how* a decision would be made. Fortunately, it may not be too late to do this. Paul could approach the key decision makers not with additional arguments for buying a system, but with a plan for evaluating the need, defining possibilities, and assessing potential options. It may be harder for the CEO and CFO to say no to a good decision-making process than to say no to a substantive proposal.

Finally, efforts to influence the process can help create action-forcing events and so move things forward. Each step of the process, beginning with needs assessment, could be tied to specific timetables and reporting requirements that will impel the process forward. Recall that action-forcing events are intended to get people to confront the need to make hard choices. Specifically, they eliminate "delay and defer" as an option and focus attention on yes/no decisions. Thus, they are a powerful tool for choice shaping. But they must also be used with care. You must be pretty sure that the balance of driving and restraining forces favors your point of view, lest the action you force be a no.

Influencing Through Multiple Channels

As Paul develops his framing and choice-shaping strategies, he also should analyze influence networks, identify potential channels for persuasion, and think hard about sequencing. As discussed in the previous chapter, the starting point is to place key decision makers in the context of their influence networks. To whom might they turn for advice on this issue? How influential might various advisers and counselors be on this issue?

Armed with this knowledge, Paul can think about whether and how to activate those potential pathways for persuasion. Does it make sense, for example, to consult with key advisers of the CEO and CFO? If so, when should he do it and in what order?

Likewise, what potential role should these channels play in his efforts to shape perceptions of interests and alternatives? Does it make sense to try to influence through multiple channels? What is the right mix of indirect influence (i.e., through advisers and counselors) and direct influence (i.e., through interactions with the key decision makers)? What is a promising sequencing strategy for doing this? Are there potential downsides to proceeding this way?

Managing Two Key Tensions

Finally, Paul has to take care to manage two key tensions as he moves forward with his efforts to learn and influence.

Planning and Improvising

The first is the tension between planning and improvising. Most of the time, you can't hope to look forward more than a few steps down the negotiating path. Negotiations are simply not predictable or linear processes. They tend to go off at right angles, becoming suddenly and surprisingly productive or unpromising, or moving in completely unpredictable directions. And when they do, they leave the best-laid plans in tatters. So once again, it pays to be judicious in deciding how much to invest in preparation and planning before you go to the table.

This is not to say, of course, that you shouldn't gather information and do some planning before going to the table. As discussed previously, it's a basic principle of negotiation that advantage goes to the negotiator who holds the information high ground. But the information high ground is captured and held as much through effective learning at the negotiating table as it is through prenegotiation preparation.

Good negotiators understand what can and cannot be learned before they go to the negotiating table, and allocate their resources accordingly. They also are self-conscious about defining what they want to learn from counterparts once they initiate talks, and craft strategies and tactics for eliciting that information. They treat learning as an integrated and ongoing process, and don't fall into the "prepare, then plan, then negotiate" trap.

Skilled negotiators likewise understand how to strike the right balance between planning influence strategies and improvising them. To be sure, they try to anticipate the direction that negotiations will take and the "moves" their counterparts will make. They also keep their eye on the ball in terms of goals and progress toward achieving them. But they know that too much planning is not only a waste, it can leave you "brittle," unprepared to deal with the inevitable surprises. Richard Holbrooke, the architect of the negotiations that ended the war in Bosnia and of numerous business deals, and one of the finest negotiators whom I had the privilege to learn from, has the following as his mantra: "Negotiating requires flexibility on tactics but a constant vision of the ultimate goal."

This definitely doesn't mean that you can simply make it up as you go along. Instead, great negotiators are like jazz musicians: they develop a repertoire of tools and techniques, as well as skill in sensing and responding to emerging patterns, and then improvise variations on well-understood themes.

Commitment and Overcommitment

The second tension involves walking the fine line between commitment and overcommitment. A key element of Paul's ability to persuade on this issue is the extent of his own commitment to it. But he has to be sure he does not become overcommitted to a failing course of action and so both lose the game and lose credibility in the process.

Commitment is, after all, contagious. The more, and the more often, Paul demonstrates that he is seriously committed to getting a new system for his sales force, the more likely he is to get it. Why? Because he is implicitly staking his existing capital and his reputation on making it happen. This means that the CEO and CFO have to increasingly factor in the damage that would be done to Paul and his standing by saying no. On the margin, then, commitment can help sway the balance.

But it's important to remember that personal commitment should never be the sole, or even the primary, driver for sticking with a negotiating position. If you don't have a winning argument, at some point it's best to stop digging your hole even deeper. The problem is that commitment, by its very nature, means you have become personally identified with achieving some outcome. So it can be very hard to let go, even as the costs of not doing so mount.

One basic principle for avoiding overcommitment was articulated by Richard Holbrooke, the key U.S. negotiator of the Dayton Accords, which ended the war in Bosnia. His maxim was, "Be firm on goals and flexible on means." If you are going to commit yourself, do so to achieving certain outcomes, and not to exactly how you are going to get there. Even with respect to outcomes, it often is wise to leave yourself some wiggle room. If you end up getting 90 percent of what you wanted, you may want to be able to declare victory.

Then, if it looks as if you are not going to win a reasonable deal, it helps if you have thought about "off-ramps" before things fall apart. Are there points at which you could, with reasonable supporting rationales, shift your position or even shift the agenda to less fraught issues? As my grandmother put it, "If at first you don't succeed, try, try again. And then give up and don't be a damned fool."

Finally, keep in mind that the same basic principles apply to helping your counterparts get themselves out from under unsustainable commitments. You can help them see, for example, that they might be able to achieve important goals (be firm on goals) in ways that they had not considered (but be flexible on means). You will also certainly face situations where it will be better to help the people on the other side of the table find face-saving ways to back away gracefully rather than force them into humiliating comedowns.

Concluding Comments

The influence strategies outlined in this chapter helped Paul secure approval for the system. He went back and made the process case for doing a deeper evaluation and for considering intermediate options. He was then able to secure approval for a limited trial of the new system with key account representatives. The success of this trial, combined with support from Elizabeth for integration of Beta's sales and production systems, ultimately carried the day, and SalesForcePlus was implemented, in its basic version, companywide. Paul was able to negotiate a multiyear payment option with the vendor, which helped overcome the CFO's concerns about cash flow. It took substantially more time than Paul would have liked, but he ultimately got most of what he wanted.

NEGOTIATOR'S CHECKLIST

How do your counterparts see their interests? What about their alternatives?

How can you learn more about their interests and alternatives? What should you do to learn away from the table and at the table?

What are promising approaches to framing (or reframing) the situation in order to influence counterparts' perceptions of their interests?

What are promising approaches to shaping counterparts' perceptions of their choices?

5

Shape the Game

EIGHTEEN MONTHS AFTER joining Beta, Paul had really hit his stride. The work he had done to strengthen the sales recruiting process, clean up the compensation system, institute first-class training, and implement new support systems had really paid off. Supported by Elizabeth's hard work on the operations side, Paul's efforts had helped Beta emerge from the turnaround. The company was back on track to sustain success.

But no good deed goes unpunished. Paul's accomplishments put him on the succession-planning radar screen at Beta. The current chief operating officer (COO) had been battling a serious illness and recently had announced his intention to retire. The CEO had made it clear that Paul was a serious contender for the COO slot. And Paul had decided he wanted to take a shot at moving up in Beta.

The upshot was some new assignments that clearly were designed to gauge Paul's executive potential. The most challenging of these was his appointment to lead a subcommittee of the board of the Medical Device Association (MDA), the industry group that represented over 90 percent of U.S. and European medical device manufacturers.

Paul's CEO had been on the board of the MDA for several years. In consultation with the rest of the board, he had nominated Paul to lead the MDA's newly formed Subcommittee on Intellectual Property (IP) Protection. The IP subcommittee had recently been established and was charged with strengthening international protections for intellectual property—in particular, by pressing to have developing countries adopt patent law systems similar to those in force in the United States, Europe, and Japan.

Patent law systems in developed countries provided strong protection—in the form of twenty-year government-granted monopolies—for inventions created by the devices industry. Thus, they provided the economic incentives necessary for companies to invest in R&D. Without patents, inventions could easily be copied and sold by others at prices too low to support innovation in the industry.

So long as most companies in the industry, including Beta, had sold their products primarily in the United States, Europe, and Japan, there was no problem. But as globalization had taken hold, new markets had opened up and new competitors had emerged in developing countries. These competitors were unrestrained by domestic law in their countries from reverse engineering and producing versions of products developed by others. The result was a rising tide of copying and outright counterfeiting.

This had begun to hurt Beta and other established players. Not only was it difficult to secure a position in rapidly growing developing-country markets, it was positively dangerous to try to do so. The company's products had been rapidly copied and sold locally. Worse, counterfeit versions—for example, of the high-margin disposable sterilization "kits" used in Beta's equipment—rapidly found their way into developed-country markets. When this happened, it both undercut Beta's profitability and created serious risks for patient safety and the associated potential for public relations disasters. By one estimate, the problem had grown to the point where U.S. medical device manufacturers were losing $3 billion in sales a year, and the problem was only going to get worse. The industry had decided it could no longer rely on governments to tackle the problem alone.

Paul's new job, then, was to help coordinate an industry campaign to get developing countries to adopt more stringent laws protecting IP. The MDA board viewed this as a high priority and was willing to devote significant resources, in the form of staff time and funding, to make it a reality. Paul's subcommittee consisted of representatives of two other companies and was supported by a full-time staff director. Paul also would be able to hire some dedicated expert resources from the outside and could potentially draw on people at member companies for short-term assignments.

The reasons why his CEO had asked him to take on this challenge rapidly became clear to Paul. The seismic shift in role from "sales warrior" to "corporate diplomat" meant negotiating a whole new world, both figuratively and literally. If he was going to help reshape the rules of the game for IP protection, Paul would first have to become conversant with key nonbusiness "rule makers" in governments, the press, nongovernmental organizations (NGOs), and industry associations, as well as in transnational organizations such as the World Trade Organization (WTO). He also would have to build and work with a cross-functional team whose expertise he did not understand

and whose abilities he did not know how to evaluate. In addition, he would be called upon to work closely with people from companies with which Beta competed aggressively in the marketplace. To win this "game," he would have to build collaborations within the industry. This was an eye-opener in and of itself for Paul—that bitter adversaries in the marketplace could simultaneously be allies when it came to shaping the rules of the game.

Success in this new assignment also would require Paul to employ a different set of negotiating skills. Recall that anytime you get to influence whether and how negotiations take place, you have opportunities to "shape the game." Once the "who" (parties) and the "what" (issues) are established, for example, that situation powerfully influences the potential to create and capture value. Likewise, early efforts to organize and build coalitions can often have major impacts on outcomes.

The implication is that you (and Paul) must think early and hard about whom you want to negotiate with and what you want to negotiate about. To the greatest extent possible, you should seek negotiating partners who share your north-star mind-set: to create value to the maximum extent possible and to capture value while sustaining relationships and reputation. Strive, within the limits of practicality, of course, to deal with "good" parties and to eliminate "bad" parties from the mix.

The issue agenda is likewise something you should try to influence from the beginning. Is it too narrow, offering too little potential for mutually beneficial trades? Is it so broad that complexity will swamp efforts to create and capture value? Does it include toxic issues that spoilers have intentionally included in an attempt to scuttle the deal? If so, then you should move aggressively to add and/or eliminate issues.

Shaping the game is therefore about influencing the players, the agenda, and perceptions of interests and alternatives very early in the process, and reshaping them as the process evolves. At this point in Paul's new assignment, the issue is not how best to conduct face-to-face interactions with other parties; it's how to initiate and sustain a promising negotiation process.

Put another way, what he needs at this stage are the skills of an architect, not a bricklayer. As Sun Tzu expressed it so vividly, "The highest form of generalship is to balk the enemy's plans; the next best is to prevent the junction of the enemy's forces; the next in order is to attack the enemy's army in the field; and the worst policy of all is to besiege walled cities."[1] Shaping the game is about proactively shaping the future and not reacting to emerging events.

In terms of the negotiation strategy matrix shown in figure 5-1, Paul must therefore shift his focus to operate in the right-hand column. Away from the negotiating table, he must figure out how to initiate promising negotiations and seek to change the structure in favorable ways through unilateral action. At the negotiating table, he must work with other players to establish the agenda, build coalitions, and further shape the context in which negotiations take place. All the while, he must build and sustain momentum toward achieving a favorable outcome for his industry and for Beta.

Establishing Goals

Before thinking about strategy, Paul should clarify his goals. The place to start in doing this is to assess whether you are playing offense or defense. Are you seeking to initiate negotiations or seeking to forestall them? Paul's goal is to change the rules

FIGURE 5-1

The negotiation strategy matrix

	Play the game	Shape the game
Away from the negotiating table	*Prepare and plan*—Diagnose the structure of the negotiation, and develop strategies that are a good match to the situation.	*Unilaterally alter the structure*—Proactively initiate negotiations; take unilateral actions to influence participations and linkages.
At the negotiating table	*Learn and influence*—Probe counterparts' perceptions of their interests and alternatives while seeking to influence their perceptions of yours.	*Negotiate the structure*—Negotiate and renegotiate participation, the agenda, deadlines, and other key elements.

for how IP is dealt with in developing countries; he is playing offense.

Initiating negotiations to make changes others oppose is a much tougher proposition than blocking changes sought by others. Blocking a change usually means preserving the status quo, and inertia is a powerful force to have on your side. As one experienced Washington lobbyist put it, "Blocking something is a lot easier than starting something. It takes a lot less energy and time to block something than it takes to build momentum to get something done. Anything new or any change takes a lot of resources, energy, and time."[2]

If, like Paul, you are playing offense, the tasks before you range from making the case for change, to garnering support, to sustaining momentum over the long haul. In Paul's situation, progress only will happen through negotiations among national governments. Paul's goal is therefore both to catalyze these negotiations and to shape the agenda for them in ways that make a favorable agreement possible. Note that the negotiations could involve a series of bilateral agreements between developed- and developing-country governments or a broader, multilateral deal. They could be narrowly focused on IP issues or be part of a broader agenda. Major changes like this can take years to bring about. So Paul will have to develop an organization and strategies that are sustainable over time.

If you are playing defense, then you will be trying to block efforts by others to achieve their goals through negotiation. When this is the case, you must further clarify your goals. Are you seeking to block negotiations outright, to shape them so that they are less harmful to you, or to delay the inevitable? Different goals demand different strategies.

- **Blocking change** is your goal if the change in question will seriously damage your interests and if you judge that outright defeat is possible.

- **Shaping change** is your goal if negotiations that are counter to your interests are clearly going to change but you can influence how they evolve, and mitigate the damage.

- **Delaying change** is the goal when an opposing coalition has formed that is too powerful to block and the best you can do is to buy some time.

You also need to be prepared to shift your goals. If you cannot accomplish your primary goal, what is your next-best option? This means keeping an eye out for signs that you need to shift your goals. For instance, it may make sense to move from blocking to shaping if you find that you are unable to prevent a negotiating process from moving forward. If you stick too unbendingly to one goal, you may overlook an opportunity to minimize damage or even gain advantage.

Crafting Strategy

Once you have defined your goals, you can draw upon an established repertoire of "game-shaping strategies" to achieve them. This means choosing promising combinations of the following elements to favorably influence the structure of your negotiations:

- **Organizing to influence.** Creating, staffing, funding, and directing organizations devoted to initiating, opposing, and influencing negotiation processes.

- **Establishing the agenda.** Defining a promising initial agenda or modifying it as the process proceeds.

- **Playing the frame game.** Crafting and promulgating a favorable framing of "the problem" in order to influence key constituencies.

- **Selecting the forum.** Identifying the most promising forum in which to pursue one's objectives (offense or defense) and then ensuring that negotiations take place there.

- **Creating coalitions.** Identifying existing and potential coalitions and then devising plans for building supportive coalitions and neutralizing or breaking blocking coalitions.

- **Leveraging linkages.** Linking and delinking sets of negotiations to increase bargaining power.

- **Building momentum.** Creating multichannel influence campaigns and setting up action-forcing events to impel the process forward.

Organizing to Influence

Paul is just one person; he can't hope to have much impact alone. So he has to identify and tap into sources of knowledge and energy in order to create momentum. The place to begin is with building a team with the right mix of expertise and getting it started doing the right research and analysis. What types of expertise are required to understand the situation and craft effective strategies? What initial research would be most helpful in providing guidance for how to proceed? What level of funding will be required to support this effort, and from where will it come?

In consultation with the two other industry representatives on the IP subcommittee and the dedicated staff director for the project, Paul developed a proposal and submitted it to the MDA board. With the approval of the board, Paul was able to get an experienced corporate relations person, recommended by the staff director, who knew his capabilities, and seconded from a member company for a one-year, full-time assignment. While there was some resistance to having this person involved full-time, Paul thought it was essential, and pressed successfully to get him fully dedicated to the project.

Paul also got authority to hire three additional people from the outside. The first was a well-recognized expert in international intellectual property rules who worked for a large software company. She had previously testified to Congress about the need to strengthen the rules, and so her position and capabilities were well understood. The second was a former British diplomat with decades of experience in international negotiations, most recently advising the European Commission on trade and investment issues. He would be the key adviser on process issues. The third was a senior person at the U.S. Commerce Department with experience working on trade promotion and extensive connections within the U.S. government.

Paul then convened the team to plan the initial background research. They agreed to pursue two initial strands of work. The IP expert and the former Commerce official would research and write a position paper on the impact of copying on the medical devices industry, and make the case for the need to strengthen IP protection. This document would be valuable in setting the agenda, in communicating with key external constituencies, and even in helping solidify support for action within the MDA itself.

At the same time, the corporate relations person, the former diplomat, and the Commerce Department person would begin to do a detailed mapping of parties and interests. The goals here were to (1) identify potential coalitions within the United States, Europe, and Japan to help get this issue to the top of the agenda, and (2) to assess potential blocking coalitions within and among developing countries.

In parallel, the team initiated fact-finding discussions with government officials in the United States and Europe with a view to gauging how important they perceived the issue to be, and to assessing the strength of the opposition. This helped build a network of contacts, but the initial conclusions were not promising. Officials were sympathetic to the industry's plight. But the MDA was just one of many groups seeking to advance its agenda with the U.S. administration and the European Commission, and by no means the most influential or important one. At the same time, developing-country opposition on this issue was perceived to be strong, with much alignment among key players, such as India and Brazil. (China was in the process of becoming a WTO member and so not yet involved.) Somewhat discouraged, Paul and the team went back to the drawing board.

Establishing the Agenda

The next step was to rethink the agenda they were trying to accomplish. Deciding what agenda to purse is equivalent to asking, Which issues will be negotiated, and which will be set aside? Will the agenda be broad and comprehensive, or will it focus on a narrow set of issues?

How the agenda is defined will have a major impact on what coalitions can be built and sustained. The broader the agenda, the more parties will see the potential to advance their interests. But of course, there is a downside; if the agenda is too broad, it may become intractable. In addition, it's possible to "overbuild" coalitions, which can result in lowest-common-denominator outcomes and so water down your efforts to advance your own interests. (See "Strategic Simplification.")

Recognizing the relationship between the agenda and potential coalitions, the former Commerce Department official suggested that they think about focusing on reaching out to other industries that also were concerned about intellectual property protection. The IP expert supported this, indicating that she thought the software industry was facing similar issues, albeit with copyright protection rather than patents. Two other key industries—pharmaceuticals and entertainment—also were obvious candidates. The former was, like the MDA, concerned about patents, while the entertainment industry was concerned about copyright protection for movies and music.

Concluding that this was a sound idea, Paul consulted with

Strategic Simplification

The full set of parties and issues, and the related set of interests and trade-offs, defines the *party-issue space* of a complex negotiation. As the numbers of parties and issues in a negotiation increase, so too do the information processing demands on negotiators. It is usually straightforward for two parties to negotiate over a single issue, whether they reach agreement or not, but what happens in a negotiation when one hundred parties sit at a table simultaneously negotiating one hundred issues?

Fortunately, complex negotiations can be transformed into two or more simpler linked subnegotiations. Useful simplification strategies include subtracting, splitting, and sequencing.

Subtracting means working to reduce the number of parties and/or issues to a tractable core. A related approach involves identifying issues that are "toxic"—that is, preventing progress from being made—and finding ways to defer or avoid dealing with them.

Splitting means taking more complex negotiations and dividing them into multiple subnegotiations. The key is to do this without eliminating too much potential for value creation. Suppose, for example, that four parties are negotiating over four issues. The following party-issue grid defines their preferences. The orientation of the arrows indicates the direction of a party's preference on a given issue, and the number of arrows indicates the relative strength of that preference. What does this grid show? It suggests that pairs of parties could engage in independent value-creating trades on pairs of issues. Parties 1 and 2 should negotiate issues 1 and 2 (subgroup A), and parties 3 and 4 should negotiate issues 3 and 4 (subgroup B).

Sequencing means dealing with parties and/or issues in some order rather than trying to deal with them all at once. Here too, the key is to do this in ways that don't eliminate the potential for value creation.

	Issue 1	Issue 2	Issue 3	Issue 4
Party 1				
Party 2	Subgroup A			
Party 3				
Party 4			Subgroup B	

Sequencing of issues and/or parties also offers rich opportunities to create momentum.

As summarized in the following table, these three simplification strategies can be applied to shaping the party structure or issue structure of negotiations.

Strategy	Party structure	Issue structure
Subtract: Eliminate elements in the party structure or issue structure.	Exclude parties.	Eliminate issues from the agenda.
Split: Divide up elements of the party structure or issue structure.	Divide the parties into two or more groups.	Divide the issues into two or more subsets.
Sequence: Decouple interactions among parties or issues and address them sequentially.	Meet with parties in a particular order.	Negotiate issues in sequence to build momentum.

his CEO and then reached out to the head of the MDA board, the CEO of one of the largest medical device companies. He asked this individual to initiate discussions with the heads of the pharmaceutical, software, and entertainment trade associations. Paul helped organize and participated in key meetings. The result was an agreement to set up an ad hoc coalition, dubbed the Intellectual Property Alliance (IPA), to pursue the goal of strengthening international IP protection and to provide funding for the effort. Paul's team would effectively be "transferred" to become the core of the IPA professional staff. Paul would remain involved as one of four members of a steering committee, one drawn from each industry. In recognition of his role in initiating the effort, he was named chairman of the group.

The team immediately went to work to do the research to support the broader agenda. This meant rewriting the position paper to analyze the costs of weak international protection for all four industries. It also meant working on a set of "core principles" for what good international standards for IP protection would look like. The former diplomat had strongly advised that they put a principled stake in the ground as early as possible to shape the agenda from the outset.

A second round of consultations with government officials in the United States and Europe suggested that they were on the right track. Officials seemed much more willing to devote time to discussion, a good signal that they thought there was potential. At the same time, the team still got the message loud and clear that there were many competing priorities. They had to find a way to move international IP protection to the top of the intergovernmental agenda.

Officials also expressed concern about exactly how the agenda could be moved forward. No existing intergovernmental negotiations were underway on this issue. And starting a new process specifically devoted to IP would be difficult—not impossible, they said, but very difficult.

Playing the Frame Game

The team digested the implications and began to think through how to move international IP protection up the agenda in the United States and Europe. The corporate relations expert, seconded by the former Commerce official, suggested that they expand their meetings beyond the executive branches (United States and European Commission) and begin to consult with key legislators and their staffs to make the case. They further suggested that the place to begin was in the U.S. Congress, in part because it would be easier to navigate than the more complex politics of the European Union, and in part because business had more direct influence over legislators in Congress than in the European Parliament. If the heads of key subcommittees in Congress could be convinced to hold hearings on the subject, this would further raise the profile and directly bring senior players in the administration into the game.

To facilitate this, an experienced Washington lobbyist was added to the team. Her immediate reaction was that before she started setting up meetings first with committee staff and then with legislators, they needed to do some work on framing the issue in ways that legislators would find compelling. This meant thinking through how the broader public could be educated about what was at stake and how this fit into the broader effort, illustrated next, to exert influence through multiple, direct and indirect channels. Without public awareness of the issue, there was little hope of capturing the attention of elected representatives. The next objective, then, was to frame the issue in ways that would spur media and public debate and so focus the attention of legislators in Congress on this issue.

The more general issue is how you can attract and hold the attention of influential but somewhat dispersed constituencies through the use of persuasive communication. Political scientist Malcolm Mitchell described effective framing as "a burning glass which collects and focuses the diffuse warmth of popular emotions, concentrating them on a specific issue."[3] Used effectively, it evokes specific mental models and so promotes "right thinking"—that is, "right" in the eyes of those doing the framing—and discredits or provides counterarguments to possible "wrong thinking." Specific approaches to framing were discussed in the previous chapter.

Led by Paul, the team engaged in some brainstorming, came up with some alternative catchphrases, and did some informal testing. The catchphrase that jumped out as most powerful was "intellectual piracy." This description was crisp and potent because it evoked images of the worst forms of plunder and illegitimacy. The supporting message was that by allowing copying to go on and not putting in place legal protections, developing countries were effectively condoning theft of the hard-won IP developed by leading companies. Developing-country governments, of course, didn't see it that way. No domestic laws were being broken, and officials there had yet to perceive any downside to allowing this copying to happen.

But the intended audience did find the argument compelling. The corporate relations person developed a series of press releases and talking points, and set up interviews with leading business, financial, and general news publications. The result was a series of stories about the growing problem. Subsequent polls revealed that awareness among opinion leaders in the public went up considerably. Organizations representing broader business interests, such as the Chamber of Commerce, began to get on the bandwagon, asking their members to discuss the issue in meetings with their local representatives.

Armed with this new ammunition, the lobbyist recommended that they try to set up meetings between senior executives in the four industries that were contributing to the IPA and key members of committee staffs in Congress. These people, she said, were as important in setting the agenda as the members themselves and were key gatekeepers. It was essential, she further asserted, that the meetings involve senior line managers in the companies, ideally top executives, since they were much more likely to get a hearing than corporate or government relations personnel.

Paul participated in several such meetings, eventually culminating in one with the chairman of the Senate Commerce Committee. Intrigued by what he heard, the committee chairman agreed to schedule hearings. The lobbyist then worked closely with the staff to shape the list of witnesses. The IPA IP expert received an important early slot, and her position paper was transformed into an effective opening statement. Officials from key departments in the administration—Commerce, Treasury, State, and the Office of the United States Trade Representative (USTR)—also appeared and acknowledged the scope of the problem.

Given the progress that had been made, Paul and the rest of the IPA team were in high spirits. They had won round one of the frame game and helped move international IP protection up the agenda.

Selecting the Forum

One thing they still lacked, however, was a forum in which to pursue negotiations. They needed to identify a high-leverage way to initiate and pursue intergovernmental negotiations on IP protections.

The issue of forum selection is important in many efforts to shape the structure of negotiations. This is because *where* a negotiation takes place often strongly affects who will participate, as well as the rules of the game, and how any resulting agreement will be enforced. For this reason, vigorous jousting can occur over not just whether negotiations take place but where.

Note that thinking about negotiating forums is as important if you are playing defense as it is if you are playing offense. It usually is easier to block or delay change in some forums than it is in others.

The team's initial advice to Paul was that they should not try to catalyze a new set of negotiations on the IP issue, but rather try to "attach" the agenda to strengthen international protections to an existing set of intergovernmental talks. They offered two rationales for adopting this approach. The first was that dedicated talks would naturally focus just on the issue of IP protection, and they thought it would be difficult to make any progress on what was still a relatively narrow agenda. Developing countries would continue to see it as a win-lose proposition, they argued, and developed countries would have little leverage to win concessions. They also pointed to the experience of a recent set of dedicated negotiations, organized by the Organization for Economic Cooperation and Development (OECD), over foreign investment. These negotiations collapsed in acrimony after being vigorously opposed by NGOs. Not even the developed countries had been able to agree on a common position, never mind convincing developing countries to open up their economies for foreign investment.

The second rationale was that the most natural forum in which to pursue stand-alone intergovernmental negotiations on IP was highly unfavorable from an industry point of view. Previous international agreements on IP had been negotiated in the World Intellectual Property Organization (WIPO), a specialized agency of the United Nations located in Vienna. While some agreements had been reached in WIPO, they were essentially toothless. Because there was no effective enforcement mechanism, WIPO was powerless to adjudicate disputes and punish violations. In addition, WIPO was, like most UN organizations, governed by the rule of one nation, one vote. Thus, the developing countries held sway to a degree disproportionate to their impact on the world economy.

The team suggested to Paul that they consider bypassing WIPO and taking their agenda to a much broader intergovernmental forum, the next round of multilateral trade negotiations in the WTO. Early meetings, called "ministerial meetings," to initiate a new round were already underway, but the agenda for the round was still in the early stages of being negotiated.

While it would unquestionably be difficult, the team argued, success in getting IP protection onto the WTO agenda would be a double blessing. First, it would provide opportunities to trade gains in strengthening IP protections off against other issues developing countries cared about, such as agricultural subsidies in Europe and the United States. Second, any resulting agreement would be subject to the much more rigorous resolution mechanism governing international trade disputes.

After in-depth consultations with his steering committee, with the leadership of the trade associations supporting the IPA, within the board of the MDA, and with sympathetic government officials, Paul gave the go-ahead to his team to pursue this strategy. The team believed they had a fighting chance. Also, if the effort failed, they would still have raised awareness and built some supportive coalitions, and could fall back and consider alternative strategies.

Creating Coalitions

Paul and the team further agreed that the goal was to win IP protection a place on the agenda for the round, and not to worry too much about the shape of a final agreement. Major rounds of trade negotiations typically took years to conclude, and the negotiations were conducted by high-level government teams. There would almost certainly be a role the IPA could play in influencing these negotiations, but it was too early to worry about planning for that.

Besides, it would be a huge accomplishment just to get IP onto the agenda. Trade negotiations had traditionally been concerned with issues such as tariffs and quotas on manufactured goods. Only recently had there been moves to broaden the trade agenda to include "trade-related" issues, such as labor standards, environmental standards, competition policy, and intellectual property. Many countries were strongly opposed to doing this, since it meant negotiating major and painful changes in domestic policy. At the same time, the gains that could be achieved by lowering tariffs had largely been achieved. The major remaining barriers to free trade and the associated expansion of global trade lay in addressing the so-called nontariff barriers.

Paul's team was therefore cautiously optimistic that the timing was right to push IP onto the agenda. The key, however, was to move quickly to build coalitions to influence the agenda-setting negotiations.

In a series of brainstorming meetings, Paul's team developed an overarching three-stage coalition-building process based on the ideas of first doing some coalition mapping to identify potential allies, opponents, and "convincibles," and then developing a promising sequencing strategy. They summarized their approach as "unify the developed countries, win over the transitional economies, and isolate the implacable opponents." This meant that they would begin by developing a core coalition consisting of the United States, Canada, members of the European Union, and Japan. Once this core coalition was in place, they would try to broaden it to include countries with rapidly developing economies, such as Korea, Taiwan, Russia, and other former communist countries. This would leave the most opposed countries, such as India and Brazil, relatively isolated and perhaps vulnerable to being pressured into accepting a deal.

With this big picture in mind, the team began to develop a strategy for the first stage, unifying the developed world, in more detail. They undertook another series of consultations with supporters in the U.S. government, principally in the Commerce Department and the Office of the USTR, and got both encouragement and cautions about potential barriers to moving forward.

One major potential stumbling block emerged from these discussions: strengthening international IP protection was still not really on the radar screen in Europe and Japan. While the USTR agreed that they would begin to press the issue more strongly with their colleagues in Europe and Japan, they were not confident that it would be enough. They strongly recommended that the IPA initiate business-to-business dialogue with counterparts in Europe and Japan with a view to getting them to influence their respective governments.

The IPA team returned, once again, to mapping out influential parties and identifying influence networks. This was translated into a strategy for a *multilevel coalition-building campaign*. U.S. government officials undertook discussions at the government-to-government level. In Europe, this included dialogue both at the level of national governments and with the European Commission. In tandem, IPA team members began to build coalitions at the business-to-business level by identifying and reaching out to influential organizations representing European and Japanese industry. These organizations, in turn, were encouraged to lobby their respective governments.

While it took some time, the strategy began to bear some fruit. Governments in Europe and Japan were beginning to pay attention, and actively began to assess the merits of pushing to include IP protection on the trade negotiation agenda. Encouraged, the IPA team asked Paul and his colleagues on the steering committee to help them mobilize a broader industry coalition in the United States. Paul reached out to the executives who sat on the boards of the pharmaceutical, software, entertainment, and medical device industry associations and encouraged them to help set up new consultative mechanisms. Ultimately, IPA staff undertook regular quarterly consultations with representatives of fifteen U.S. industry associations to review progress and solicit input.

While this was encouraging, success in catalyzing serious government-to-government dialogue among developed countries almost immediately hit some roadblocks. It emerged that there actually were significant differences of opinion among the United States, Europe, and Japan about what a "good" international IP regime would look like. In part, this was the result of different legal traditions and standards of protection. Should patents be granted, for example, to the first to file for a patent or the first to invent a technology? In addition, strengthening protection in "sensitive" industries—for example, entertainment—posed particular challenges because some European governments viewed them as having special cultural status.

If these differences of opinion could not be managed, it would be difficult to sustain a coalition in the face of concerted opposition from developing countries. Paul and the team went back into brainstorming mode. What emerged was a variation on the "focus first on principles and then on details" approach to building momentum. Rather than try to thrash out the details of what an eventual agreement might look like, developed-country governments could agree to pursue a specific set of principles. Rather than argue, for example, over whether the patent system would be first-to-file or first-to-invent, for example, they agreed to push for the principle that "every country has to have a system for giving and enforcing patents." Only when the coalition had won the battle and IP was on the agenda for the next round, would they engage in hard bargaining over the specifics.

To support this effort, the IP expert on the team wrote a new position paper, "Principles for International Intellectual Property Protection." Carefully researched and extensively communicated to interested parties, this document helped seal agreement among key developing-country governments to strongly putting IP onto the trade agenda. It later became the basis for negotiating the eventual agreement in "trade-related intellectual property" (TRIPS) in the WTO.

Leveraging Linkages

With the developed-country government and industry coalitions coming together, the IPA team could begin to strategize on how to broaden them to include "middle ground" players, such as Korea, Taiwan, Indonesia, and Russia. The key here was to figure out how to shape their perceptions of both their interests and their alternatives so that supporting putting IP on the agenda would be palatable.

The key to doing this turned out to be setting up and leveraging some linked negotiations. As discussed previously, various types of linkage—competitive and interdependent, sequential and simultaneous—can powerfully influence parties' perceptions of their interests and alternatives. So the key was to think through what sorts of linkages might be helpful.

The answer turned out to be to encourage the U.S. government to undertake some bilateral negotiations with key governments in order to help build momentum behind putting IP on the agenda for multilateral trade talks. The former Commerce official highlighted for the team that an instrument already existed for putting pressure on specific governments about trade issues. The 1974 Trade Act had included provisions, known as Section 301, that allowed the United States to effectively impose sanctions on governments that engaged in unfair trading practices.

However, these provisions had never been applied to intellectual property issues and probably couldn't be unless additional supporting legislation was passed. Drawing on the close connections the IPA had established with congressional staff and the growing perception of the magnitude of the problem, IPA convinced key legislators to introduce a bill that would make intellectual property rights actionable under Section 301. The bill further made "adequate and effective" IP protection a condition for eligibility under what was known as the Generalized System of Preferences—trade law provisions that had allowed the United States to give special market access to developing countries. If the bill passed, the U.S. government would be able to deny other countries these benefits if they didn't play ball on IP. In addition, the bill proposed the creation of the position of assistant USTR for international investment and intellectual property. This meant there would be a piece of the bureaucracy whose mission it was to monitor IP issues and report to Congress.

Although it took several months, there was little opposition, and the bill was passed and signed into law. Once the new assistant USTR was named, IPA attention turned to encouraging the expeditious use of the new tools to advance the IP agenda. After a period of investigation, the U.S. government decided to launch a Section 301 case, with the first target being Korea, an ideal target because of its economic reliance on exporting to the United States. Using the threat of sanctions as leverage, the United States negotiated a bilateral agreement on intellectual property with Korea. In another example of linkage, this agreement eventually became a model for a comprehensive multilateral TRIPS agreement.

Buoyed by this success, the USTR placed several other governments on an intellectual property "watch list," signaling that they too could be the subject of Section 301 actions and even sanctions. The resulting chill altered many governments' views about the desirability of negotiating an international agreement on IP issues. Better, they began to think, to have an international agreement with a solid, impartial enforcement mechanism, than to have the most powerful economic player in the world targeting countries on a more ad hoc, politically motivated basis.

The net effect of this linkage of bilateral and multilateral negotiations was to turn the tide in terms of winning broader international support for getting IP on the agenda. What remained was to formally negotiate inclusion of IP on the agenda at the ministerial meeting that would formally launch the new round. This would mean overcoming the opposition of the remaining, most implacable opponents.

Building Momentum

The final approach to shaping the structure involved finding ways to build momentum in favorable directions. A number of such strategies have already been discussed, including the use of multiple influence channels and multilevel coalition-building strategies to influence key decision makers, as well as focusing on overarching principles rather than details, and using sequencing tactics.

The principal momentum-building tool that remains to be discussed is *action-forcing events*. Recall that these are events, such as deadlines, meetings, and even actions in linked negotiations, that force other players to confront the need to make hard decisions. They can be *negotiated* (e.g., a deadline mutually agreed on by the negotiators), *unilateral* (e.g., a threat tied to a deadline), or *externally imposed* (i.e., arising from outside circumstances beyond the control of negotiators). Regardless, they act as break points at which negotiators must make a move to avoid incurring substantial and irreversible costs.

In this situation, the ministerial meeting that had been scheduled to launch the round was the key action-forcing event. The IPA had to be sure that the U.S. government made inclusion of IP on the agenda a condition for starting the round. All the hard work to build and sustain the developed-country government and business coalitions paid off here.

Consulting closely with key government officials and keeping up the pressure through the broader network of trade associations, the IPA won a commitment that the United States would not agree to launch the round without IP being included on the agenda.

That commitment, combined with the success in pressuring middle-ground countries, meant that the remaining holdouts, such as India and Brazil, were isolated and faced a very tough choice. They could allow the negotiations to launch the round to fail (by the consensus rules of the WTO, all parties had to agree to move forward) and put at risk all the potential gains in other dimensions of trade, or they could accede. Faced with the action-forcing event, they gave ground, and IP was placed on the agenda for the round.

While it took several more years, the agreement that emerged from this round enshrined a high set of standards for intellectual property protection in international trade law. It compelled all member countries to create systems compatible with basic principles very close to those the IPA had put forward. While some flexibility was granted concerning timing for implementation, the agreement was a huge win for the IPA and for businesses concerned about protecting and profiting from their intellectual property.

By participating in this process, Paul learned some invaluable lessons that served him well when he was appointed to be Beta's new COO. One fundamental takeaway concerned his responsibility to proactively work to shape the competitive environment in which his business operated. A second concerned the need to both compete with and cooperate with other companies in his industry. A third concerned the power of sustained efforts to build coalitions to influence government and the public environment, and the surprising value of people who knew how to conduct this "corporate diplomacy."

Concluding Comments

Paul acquired a potent toolbox of techniques to shape the game in negotiations. This paid dividends, not just in subsequent efforts to influence the public environment but also in high-stakes negotiations with customers and a major acquisition that Beta undertook a year after Paul was named COO. He was able to think coherently about how to organize to influence, establish the agenda, play the frame game, select the right forums, create coalitions, leverage linkages, and build momentum in these and a host of other negotiations. These skills continued to serve him well when, three years later, the CEO retired and named Paul his successor.

Negotiator's Checklist

How should you organize to influence the process?

What forum would be most advantageous in which to conduct the negotiations?

How can you influence the agenda?

What are the most promising coalitions for you to build? Which should you try to prevent from forming? Which might you need to break?

How is this negotiation linked to other negotiations? What linkages should you try to create? Which should you try to prevent?

Who are key audiences and what are promising framing strategies? How are your adversaries likely to try to frame the issues?

What can you do to channel the flow of the negotiation process? Would it be helpful to set up deadlines or other action-forcing events? How do you avoid being pressured into making a commitment before you want to?

6

Organize to Improve

IN MAKING THE JOURNEY from prospective candidate for VP of sales to CEO of Beta Corporation, Paul encountered a rich range of negotiating situations—dealing with bosses, peers, direct reports, as well as internal and external stakeholders. As such, his experience is a representative snapshot of the diverse negotiations you typically will encounter in transitioning into new roles.

Thus far, we have drawn on Paul's experience to develop a framework that will help you better manage each negotiating change you face in transitioning into a new role. You should now feel well equipped to:

- Diagnose distinct types of negotiations and match strategy to situation.

- Learn and influence in face-to-face interactions with counterparts at the negotiating table.

- Shape the game in ways that set the stage for productive interactions and favorable outcomes.

In doing this, we have, however, glossed over a very critical driver of Paul's success: *he got better at negotiating over time.* By the time Paul was appointed to CEO of Beta, he was a much more skilled negotiator than when he first joined the company. He was able to manage more and more complex negotiations and consistently achieve better outcomes. Our final major theme, then, is that the ability to learn is itself a source of advantage in negotiation (and, more generally, in making successful transitions into new roles).

What do we mean by *learning*? We have already discussed the importance of one type of learning in negotiation—the ability to gain information about counterparts' needs and wants, drivers, and resistance points—in chapter 4. This type of learning is, of course, a critical driver of success in every negotiation you conduct. If you gain more insight into your counterparts—through prenegotiation preparation and at the table—than they do into you, you will sustain an informational advantage. This may permit you to overcome other disadvantages or to cement a dominant position. Regardless, superior capacity for this type of learning is a precious asset.

In this chapter, however, we will focus on a different sort of learning: the ability to get better at negotiating through a disciplined focus on personal and organizational improvement. Why is this important? Because small enhancements in your ability to learn and improve in every negotiation you conduct can yield very big net increases in effectiveness over time. It's like compound interest. Invest $10,000 at 5 percent per annum, and you have $16,288 after ten years. Increase the interest rate to 10 percent, and you get $25,937 for the same initial investment. It is for this reason that we made "organize to improve" the fourth of the strategic imperatives introduced in chapter 2 and illustrated in figure 6-1.

FIGURE 6-1

Strategic imperatives

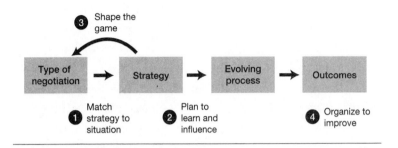

Nature and Nurture

A story is told of an eminent geneticist who is asked by a student whether nature or nurture is more important in shaping human behavior. "Nature wins," he confidently replied, "51 percent to 49 percent."

So it is with negotiating ability. The answer to the question, Are great negotiators born or made? turns out to be yes. Yes, you sit somewhere on a spectrum of innate negotiating talent, and yes, you can develop your talent to a greater or lesser degree. Seen in this light, it is pointless to worry about nature versus nurture. Of course both matter. But the reality is that there isn't much you can do at this point on the nature side; you should focus on nurturing the talent you have.

Put another way, everyone can learn to be a better negotiator. The more interesting question, therefore, is not Are great negotiators born or made? but rather How best do we develop negotiating ability? To answer this question, we need to probe what contributes to the development of expertise. How does the expert mind differ from the novice mind? What mental capacities do skilled negotiators have that are absent in their less accomplished colleagues? How might such capacities be enhanced?

The nature-versus-nurture discussion also misses a critical point that we have emphasized throughout the book: that there are many different types of negotiations. The stereotypical portrait of a "great" negotiator is the poker player who is able to parlay weak hands into wins at the table through the use of charisma, threat, and bluff. But is such a person likely to be great at all types of negotiation? The answer is definitively no. This sort of style works well when negotiations are primarily about capturing value and when the negotiator is a principal who doesn't have to worry much about internal decision making and ratification.

The implication is that you are likely to be better at some types of negotiation than at others. Are you more effective at creating value or at capturing value? Are you more comfortable in deal making or dispute resolution? Do you prefer more one-shot, transactional situations or negotiating in the context of ongoing relationships? As you begin to design your own plan for improvement, you should therefore think hard about *what kinds* of negotiations you want to get better at conducting. This will help you better focus on the specific sets of skills you want to acquire or enhance.

Art and Science

Then there is the question of whether negotiation is an art or a science. This is important because it has major implications for how one should approach becoming a better negotiator. And as with the nature-versus-nurture debate, the answer turns out to be yes. More precisely, it turns out that negotiation is an art whose practice often is supported by "science," in the form of various sorts of economic, legal, and behavioral analysis.

The focus of the remainder of this chapter will be on learning the art part of effective negotiating. This is not to say, however, that the science is unimportant; often it is terribly important. It's just that the science is both easier to learn and easier to get help with—in the form of advisers—than the art of negotiating. The good news about learning about science is that key ideas can be reduced to written principles, methodologies, and tools. The recommend reading section at the end of the book highlights some general resources on the analytics of negotiation.

To go much beyond this, though, you should, once again, keep the type of negotiation in which you are engaged firmly in mind. This is because myriad forms of economic, legal, and behavioral analysis potentially can support various types of negotiations. If Paul were engaged in a difficult labor-management negotiation at one of Beta's plants, for example, he would be well advised to have people on his team who understood the complexities of labor law, and who could develop models of the economics of the employment relationship. On the behavioral analysis side, it could help to have advisers who were conversant with the research on the dynamics of unions as political and social entities, and the roles of leaders within them. None of this would be much help, though, if Paul were negotiating a major acquisition.

Novices and Experts

How can one best learn the art of negotiating? This is an instance of the much broader issue of how people become experts who are able to navigate effectively in complex, fuzzy, shifting, unstructured environments. Research on naturalistic decision making—the way people make decisions—suggests that experts manage such environments vastly better than novices.[1] They do so because of their superior abilities in five key areas: pattern recognition, mental simulation, parallel processing, robust response, and reflection-in-action:

- *Pattern recognition* is the ability to see actionable patterns in complex and confusing negotiating situations.[2] Like expert chess players, skilled negotiators filter out irrelevant clutter and see configurations that represent threats and opportunities.

- *Mental simulation* is the ability to rapidly come up with promising courses of action and then simulate them forward in time in the imagination. In this way, skilled negotiators anticipate the reactions of other players, develop promising action sequences, think through potential contingencies, and progressively refine or discard the plan as necessary.

- *Parallel processing* is what Roland Christensen described as the "dual competency" of managing substance and process in tandem. It permits the expert negotiator to keep track of the substance of negotiations while observing and shaping the evolution of the process.[3]

- *Robust response* is the ability rapidly to develop workable options under time pressure. Rather than work out detailed plans far into the future, the expert looks ahead a few moves, designs strategies that are not "brittle"—in the sense of needing a lot of variables all to be aligned—and anticipates making rapid adjustments as events unfold.

- *Reflection-in-action* is the ability for the negotiator to, as William Ury so aptly put it in *Getting Past No,* "go to the balcony" in the midst of tense and difficult proceedings, get perspective on what is happening and why, and adjust strategies accordingly.[4]

Becoming an expert in negotiation, then, is about honing these five abilities in the context of the specific types of negotiating situations you will face.

The research further suggests that you can accelerate the development of expertise by (1) gaining exposure to a diverse range of realistic situations, both real negotiations and simulated ones, and (2) allowing yourself to reflect on the experience and absorb the lessons. As Gary Klein put it in *Sources of Power,* his book on naturalistic decision making: "The part of intuition that involves pattern matching and recognition of . . . typical cases can be trained. If you want people to size up situations quickly and accurately, you need to expand their experience base. One way is to arrange for a person to receive more difficult cases . . . Another approach is to develop a training program, perhaps with exercises and realistic scenarios, so the person has a chance to size up numerous situations very quickly."[5]

The upshot is that your personal development program should include both structured attention to learning from experience and more formal training in negotiation technique.

Commit to Learning Disciplines

The first step in creating your "negotiator fitness plan" is a personal commitment to engage in disciplined learning during and after every significant negotiation you undertake. Negotiations seldom flow smoothly from start to finish. Instead, there often are pauses or breaks in the action. These are the times to engage in a modest amount of in-the-flow reflection about what is going on.

To make this focused and efficient, you should have a basic framework for engaging in this reflection. The negotiation strategy matrix provides a good point of departure; using it will also help you internalize the framework. Sample questions that you might ask in each cell of the matrix are summarized in table 6-1. Use them as a place to start developing your own reflection template. Consider capturing your observations in a journal, since they also will be useful when you engage in post-negotiation assessment.

After each negotiation, set aside the time, even if it's just twenty or thirty minutes, to engage in a disciplined postmortem. Start with the following general questions:

- Did this go well or poorly?

- If well, what contributed to this?

- If poorly, why, and what might I have done differently?

- What was surprising about this negotiation?

- What were the key turning points?

Next, deepen your assessment by returning to the north-star negotiation goals developed in the introduction and asking the following questions about the outcome:

- Concerning value creation:
    - Did I create value to the greatest extent possible?
    - If opportunities to create more joint value were missed, why did this happen?

TABLE 6-1

Reflection template

	Play the game	Shape the game
Away from the negotiating table	***Preparation and planning***	***Unilateral game-changing moves***
	• Do you have a clear view of the situation?	• Are there opportunities to take unilateral actions to advantageously alter the structure?
	• Have you engaged in sufficient preparation, or is there additional cost-effective information gathering that you should do?	
	• Do you understand who has or could have influence on the outcome and what their interests and alternatives are?	• Have you done all you can to develop the strongest possible alternatives?
		• Is it possible to invite new players into the game in ways that will help you advance your objectives?
	• Is the agenda a promising one, neither too broad nor too narrow?	• Are there opportunities to create advantageous linkages?
	• Are linkages creating barriers to moving forward?	• Have you done all you can to create supportive coalitions and avoid the formation of opposing ones?
	• Are there forces that will create and sustain momentum?	• Are there opportunities to create momentum through the use of action-forcing events?
At the negotiating table	***Learning and influencing***	***Negotiating (and renegotiating) the structure***
	• Is there more you can do to learn about your counterparts' needs and wants?	• Are there opportunities to enlarge or trim the agenda in order to create more joint value?
	• Do you have a clear sense of their key drivers and resistance points? What can you do to gain more clarity?	

(continued)

TABLE 6-1 (*continued*)

	Play the game	Shape the game
At the negotiating table	***Learning and influencing*** • Have you shared an appropriate amount of information about your priorities? Have they? • Are you being effective at framing the stakes? • Are your positions and concessions supported by plausible rationales? Are theirs? • Are you being effective at influencing their perceptions of their choices?	***Negotiating (and renegotiating) the structure*** • Would it help to break the agenda down into pieces that can be dealt with in parallel? • Would it help to negotiate the addition of new parties or to convince some to be represented by others? • Would it help to shift back to discussion of principles or renegotiate the process? • Would a mutual commitment to a deadline help create momentum?

- Are there things that I might have done differently?

- Are there approaches with which I will experiment the next time I am in a similar situation?

• Concerning value capture:

- Did I capture an appropriate share of the value that was created?

- Did I capture too much value, creating a situation that will jeopardize the sustainability of the deal? If so, why did this happen? How will I avoid doing this in the future?

- Did I capture too little value, creating a big pie, but letting my counterparts eat too much of it? If so, why did this happen? How will I avoid doing this in the future?

• Concerning relationships:
- Did the negotiation strengthen (or at a minimum maintain) critical relationships?
- If not, could the relationship damage have been avoided?
- If the damage could have been avoided, what did I do to unnecessarily damage the relationship? How might I avoid doing this in the future?

• Concerning reputation:
- Did the negotiation enhance (or at least not diminish) my reputation as a "tough, creative, and trustworthy" negotiator?
- If not, could I have avoided damaging my reputation? If so, was there more that I could have done to enhance my reputation?
- If damage could have been avoided, how should I have acted differently? How might I avoid similar problems in the future?

The next step is to revisit the assessments you made—using the negotiation strategy matrix template of questions in table 6-1—of the negotiation process and your efforts to shape it. Here too, try to distill out the core lessons. What went well and why in each cell of the matrix? What didn't, and what are the implications for what I will do and try in the future?

Invest in Skill Development Programs

Skill development programs are the second pillar of your personal negotiator fitness program. Why are they important? Why isn't it enough to learn from experience? For two key reasons. First, if you are only learning from experience, you can only learn at the rate you get experience. Even if you are negotiating for a living, each negotiation takes time—think of it as cycle time—and that limits your rate of improvement. Good training provides condensed experience, and this accelerates personal development.

Second, negotiations come in such a wide range of sizes and shapes that it can be difficult to draw general lessons without a conceptual framework to "organize" your experience. Otherwise, you risk developing a characteristic style that works well in some situations but not in others. Worse still, you may not understand that this is the case. This is why exposure to a good mix of concepts and simulated experience—in the form of cases, stories, and exercises—can be so powerful.

Note, however, that it is essential to participate in programs that deliver a "good" mix of concepts and simulated negotiations. And in my experience, these are few and far between. I've asked participants in the programs I teach, "What other negotiation training have you experienced?" and "What about it was good and not good?"

The results of my (admittedly unscientific) polling are not very encouraging. A lot of negotiation training is going on out there. Some of it is very good, but much of it is quite mediocre and even damaging.

What makes the difference between good and not-so-good negotiation training? It comes down to a few key characteristics:

- **Having a coherent organizing framework.** Avoid programs that have either a simplistic, one-size-fits-all view of negotiation or a framework that is too complex to help real-world practitioners diagnose their situations and gain actionable insights. In the best negotiation programs, the conceptual framework provides a scaffold on which you continue to "hang" your experience long after the program ends.

- **Being taught by people with a strong mix of theoretical grounding in the research on negotiation, practical experience in conducting real-world negotiations, and good facilitation skills.** This is a rare and precious mix. More common are programs taught either by people with little real-world negotiating experience or by practitioners with a propensity to elevate their war stories to the level of universal principles. (I should note in passing that I've become a much better teacher of negotiation since I began running my own business and am now doing much more negotiating with customers and doing alliance and licensing deals.)

- **Making extensive use of scenarios, simulation exercises, and reflection.** Part of what makes negotiation an art is that you can't tell people how to diagnose and develop good strategies; they have to experience novel situations, struggle, experiment, reflect, and learn. To return to Gary Klein's work on the development of expertise, "A good simulation can sometimes provide more training value than direct experience. A good simulation lets you stop the actions, back up and see what went on, and cram many trials so a person can

develop a sense of typicality."[6] For this to happen, of
course, you have to experience good scenarios and
exercises, and you have to have a skilled facilitator who
helps you reflect on the experience and distill out key
insights.

- **Giving participants a reasonable amount of personalized
  attention.** Too many negotiation programs are set up
  as high-throughput assembly lines. Large numbers of
  people are gathered in a room and put through a stan-
  dardized experience. This *can* be better than nothing.
  But it doesn't compare in terms of impact to programs
  involving small numbers of people who get some personalized attention. As you evaluate programs, ask
  whether they involve (1) any opportunities for analysis
  of specific negotiation situations you are experiencing
  or have experienced and/or (2) any personalized feed-
  back on your negotiation style—for example, in the
  form of being recorded on video and having program
  staff discuss how you did.

- **Lasting long enough to have a sustained impact on habits
  of mind.** In my experience, this means a minimum of
  three solid days, and ideally a week. Otherwise, you risk
  having a superficial experience from which little will
  truly stick. In the midst of a busy schedule, this may
  seem like a lot of time to invest. But think of it this way.
  If the program makes you just 5 percent better in every
  negotiation in which you engage from that point
  onward, what is it worth to you?

Finally, don't forget to take some time at the end of any program in which you participate to incorporate the key learnings

into the templates you use to reflect on and learn from future negotiations.

Drive Organizational Improvement

If you oversee the work of groups of negotiators, you also should strive to instill the same sorts of improvement disciplines in them. The organizations that do this best, unsurprisingly, are negotiation intensive. They include private equity companies, merger-and-acquisition advisory firms, foreign ministries, and sales organizations, such as the one Paul built when he became VP of sales at Beta. The ability to negotiate is a distinct competence for them. They recognize it and invest in building it.

But it's a challenge, even for the best of organizations led by people with the best of intentions, to make organizational learning happen. To understand why, we must distinguish between the different types of knowledge. As illustrated in table 6-2, knowledge can be explicit or tacit, as well as individual or relational.[7] The explicit-versus-tacit knowledge distinction is illustrated by the differences in how people are trained to be physicists and artists. The prospective physicist reads about mathematics and science, attends lectures in her field, and solves problems that have right and wrong answers. Much of the knowledge she must acquire is explicit—meaning it can be written down as rules, laws, and procedures, and can be transmitted from more-knowledgeable to less-knowledgeable people through books, papers, lectures, and seminars.

By contrast, and as discussed earlier, the prospective artist learns largely by doing—by making art herself—and by being coached by experienced "masters." Much of the knowledge he must acquire is tacit—it cannot be written down as rules, laws, and procedures, so it can't easily be transferred from a more experienced person to a less experienced person in written or verbal form. In fact, master artists sometimes are not able to articulate their own recipe for success. They only know good work when they see it.

The second key distinction—between individual knowledge and relational knowledge—can be understood by thinking about what it takes to build great baseball and basketball teams. One can put together an excellent baseball team by picking the best players in the major league for each position. Because baseball players operate relatively independently from one another, the resulting all-star baseball team can be expected to perform well. No matter whom they're playing with, good batters are good batters, and good fielders remain good fielders.

TABLE 6-2

Types of organizational knowledge

	Individual (Knowledge of how to do one's own work)	Relational (Knowledge of how to work effectively as part of a group)
Explicit (Transferable verbally or through writing)	• Rules • Laws • Procedures • The "science" of a profession	• Organizational charts • Formal decision-making processes • Plans for coordination • Written communication protocols
Tacit (Transferable by being shown or working with someone who has experience)	• Rules of thumb • Techniques • Approaches to individual decision making and problem solving • The "art" of a profession	• Approaches to group decision making and problem solving • Negotiated divisions of responsibility • Key sources of information and influence • Trust and credibility

In baseball, individual knowledge is much more important than relational knowledge.

But if you selected star players from the National Basketball Association for each position, would you end up with a great team? Not likely. Basketball involves a high level of interdependence among team members; thus, relational knowledge is critical. Superior basketball teams play well because the players have learned to integrate their skills and develop shared "playbooks" through a great deal of practice. The stars might simply get in each other's way, making the whole much less than the sum of its parts.

This has direct, but difficult, implications for what it takes to make shared learning happen in negotiation-intensive organizations:

- The tacit knowledge gained by individual negotiators is more difficult for an organization to capture than explicit knowledge.

- Relational knowledge gained by teams or groups dealing with complex negotiations is more difficult to capture than individuals' insights into their pieces of the puzzle.

- Tacit relational knowledge—the knowledge that individuals have, but cannot easily articulate, about how to work together—is arguably the most valuable type of knowledge and the most difficult to preserve.

Organizations often fail to learn because they lack the mechanisms needed to share and codify, to the degree possible, key insights gained from the experience of individuals and teams. Such failures may occur because the organization is in a state of overload. Organizations in a reactive, "firefighting" mode can become trapped in a permanent state of crisis response that impedes learning.

Organizational learning can also suffer from what are known as *collective-action problems*. Everyone would be better off if everyone invested in sharing insights. But no one has the incentive to make the personal investments necessary to promote this learning. Everyone just hopes that someone else is doing it.

Given the challenges, what can you do to develop superior negotiating capability in your organization? The following five actions are a good place to begin:

- **Adopt shared languages.** If they are adopted organization-wide, good negotiation training programs not only upgrade organizational capability, they provide a common language for negotiators to organize to conduct negotiations and share insights. Once again, though, it is essential that you find a program that meets the criteria laid out earlier. Otherwise, you could be institutionalizing mediocrity.

- **Institutionalize apprenticeship.** As with most arts, one of the best ways to learn, in an organizational setting, is to have the novices learn from the masters in apprenticeship-like relationships. Most negotiation-intensive organizations have formal or informal apprenticeship systems. Typically, the younger and less experienced aspiring negotiators spend considerable time in supporting analytical roles, often as part of teams working for the lead negotiators. This both schools the novices in the core analytical methods and provides a low-risk environment in which they can observe and learn from the work of the masters. Eventually, if they prove worthy, they graduate to become full members of their respective guilds. Apprenticeship-like systems of this sort have been institutionalized in organizations ranging from Wall Street investment banks to the U.S. State Department.

- **Mandate postmortems.** To overcome the tendency for people to skip the learning step, you must mandate that negotiation postmortems occur, and back this up with suitable rewards and sanctions. Being too busy to learn is a death spiral. But it is a challenge to overcome the powerful forces that act to prevent disciplined reflection and sharing of the resulting insights. It therefore is essential for leaders to "walk the talk," providing living incarnations of the desired learning disciplines. It also is essential to periodically do some quality-control checks to ensure that the processes are being given more than lip service.

- **Use common templates.** In a study that Robert Aiello and I did of the negotiation systems employed by private equity firms, we found that the best systematically incorporated the results of postnegotiation analysis into written guidelines. These "negotiation templates" often consisted of checklists that were used to guide deal screening and due diligence. Critically, the templates were "live," meaning that someone was held accountable for updating and improving them.[8]

- **Align incentives.** Finally, organizational learning won't occur if individuals lack the incentives to invest and contribute to it. But achieving this incentive alignment is easier in some organizations than in others. In private equity firms, the partners have shared incentives to see the firm do well, and this makes it easier to institutionalize efforts to upgrade collective negotiation capability. This is also typically the case in foreign ministries, where "the national interest" is what these organizations are set up to advance. But it is much more of a challenge in other negotiation-intensive organizations. In sales organizations, for example, salespeople often are explicitly or implicitly competing with each other to achieve sales goals and win monetary rewards and advancement. Unsurprisingly, this creates difficult-to-surmount barriers to knowledge sharing. The only way to overcome these barriers is to adjust the incentive system to make it worthwhile for the best negotiators to invest in collective capability building.

Concluding Comments

Of the four strategic negotiation imperatives we have discussed, *organize to improve* is the toughest one to make happen. The barriers to learning, both individual and organizational, are formidable. In the rush of day-to-day events, it's terribly easy for the "investment in improvement" task to fall to the bottom of your to-do list.

This is a problem but also an opportunity, because if you can make it work, for yourself and for your organization, you will create a sustainable source of competitive advantage. The very fact that it is so difficult makes the ability to learn and improve so valuable. In modern work on business strategy, difficult-to-imitate capabilities are now seen as one of the few sources of sustainable competitive advantage. In a static world, everyone inevitably ends up at roughly the same place.

Negotiator's Checklist

Have you established a personal discipline for reflecting during negotiations?

Are you consistently engaging in rigorous postmortems after each significant negotiation?

Have you invested in identifying and participating in good negotiation training programs?

If you are leading a negotiation-intensive organization, what are you doing to upgrade its capabilities?

What can you do to drive organizational learning? Would it help to adopt a shared language? To mandate postmortems? To create shared and updated common templates? To align incentives?

Conclusion

To succeed in making transitions into challenging new positions, you have to be effective at negotiating. New leaders quite literally negotiate their new roles. Critical sources of energy into which you need to tap—your boss, your team, your peers, and stakeholders—won't mobilize themselves. You have to activate them and convince them to help advance your priorities. Skill in negotiating, and its close cousins, influencing and building coalitions, is therefore the single most important skill new leaders need to cultivate.

The four strategic imperatives developed in this book provide a firm foundation for effective negotiation in the broad range of situations confronting new leaders. Start with a thorough diagnosis of the situation, identifying the key parties, issues, levels of negotiating, and linkages. Then *match your strategy to the situation*. Critically, recognize that there is no one-size-fits-all approach to negotiating.

Once you are engaged in face-to-face discussions with counterparts, remember to *plan to learn and influence*. How do your counterparts perceive their interests and alternatives? What are their needs, as distinct from their wants? What constraints do they confront? What do they care about, and what trades might they be willing to make? Use this learning, as well as your self-analysis of your interests and alternative to frame what is at stake and influence others' perceptions in favorable ways.

As you move through your transition, be sure to anticipate the negotiations you will need to conduct and *shape the game.* Recall that the ability to influence the structure is a skill that differentiates great negotiators from good ones. This means influencing who will be involved and setting the agenda to enhance opportunities to create value and capture value. It also means doing this through unilateral action away from the table and through at-the-table negotiating.

In the process, don't lose sight of the importance of *organizing to improve* your negotiation capabilities, both individually and organizationally. Strive to create the personal disciplines and supporting templates for engaging in in-process reflection and post-negotiation analysis. If you are leading a negotiation-intensive organization, seek to overcome the barriers that stand in the way of organizational learning by establishing shared languages, institutionalizing apprenticeships, mandating postmortems, creating common templates, and aligning incentives.

Finally, enjoy the experience of learning to be a better negotiator. The skills described in this book are by no means easy to master. It takes discipline, time, and a reasonable tolerance for frustration to become a better negotiator. But the benefits of doing so are great, both for you and for the negotiations you lead. Not only will you be able to make a more effective transition to your next new role, you will do better in every future negotiation you experience.

Notes

Introduction

1. In their seminal work on negotiation, Richard Walton and Robert McKersie made the important distinction between distributive and integrative bargaining. They also noted that negotiators may engage in a mix of distributive and integrative bargaining, which they termed *mixed-motive;* see R. E. Walton and R. B. McKersie, *A Behavioral Theory of Labor Negotiations: An Analysis of a Social Interaction System* (New York: McGraw-Hill, 1965), chapters 2, 3, 4, and 5. In *The Art and Science of Negotiation,* Howard Raiffa further laid the analytical foundations for understanding the value creation and value distribution aspects of multi-issue negotiations (Cambridge, MA: Belknap Press of Harvard University Press, 1982). In *The Manager as Negotiator,* David Lax and Jim Sebenius reconceptualized mixed-motive bargaining. They viewed negotiation as embodying "creating value" and "claiming value" processes that go on in parallel: "Negotiators should focus on the dynamic aspects of negotiation, the process of creating and claiming value" (p. 254). "Value creating and value claiming are linked parts of negotiation. Both processes are present. No matter how much creative problem-solving enlarges the pie, it still must be divided; value that has been created must be claimed" (p. 33). See D. A. Lax and J. K. Sebenius, *The Manager as Negotiator* (New York: Free Press, 1987).

2. S. Matthews and M. Watkins, "Strategic Deal-making at Millennium

Pharmaceuticals," Case 800-032. (Boston: Harvard Business School Publishing, 2000), 12.

3. R. Gallucci, interview with author, Cambridge, MA, August 2000.

Chapter 1

1. For an early effort to characterize the structure of negotiations, see chapter 1 of H. Raiffa, *The Art and Science of Negotiation* (Cambridge, MA: Belknap Press of Harvard University Press, 1982). For a more developed framework, see J. K. Sebenius, "Negotiation Analysis: A Characterization and Review," *Management Science* 38 (1992): 18–38. This framework builds on the one presented in M. Watkins, "Shaping the Structure of Negotiations," Program on Negotiation Monograph M98-1, Program on Negotiation at Harvard Law School, 1998.

2. In *Getting to Yes,* Roger Fisher and William Ury highlighted the importance of focusing on alternatives. A negotiator should always seek to clarify what they would do if no agreement is possible, and also work to strengthen their alternatives. Fisher and Ury coined the term BATNA, for Best Alternative to a Negotiated Agreement, to elevate this idea. The concept is a very important one, but I find the term BATNA to be awkward and hence don't use it. See R. Fisher, W. Ury, and B. Patton, *Getting to Yes: Negotiating Agreement Without Giving In,* 2nd ed. (New York: Penguin Books, 1991).

3. William Ury, *Getting Past No: Negotiating with Difficult People* (New York: Bantam Books, 1991).

4. R. J. Aiello and M. D. Watkins, "The Fine Art of Friendly Acquisition," *Harvard Business Review,* November–December 2000.

5. Roger Fisher and William Ury made the crucial distinction between positions and interests. See Fisher, Ury, and Patton, *Getting to Yes.* For an in-depth discussion of overcommitment and other biases in decision making and their impact on negotiations, see M. H. Bazerman and M. A. Neale, *Negotiating Rationally* (New York: Free Press, 1992).

6. As David Lax and Jim Sebenius put it, "Value creating and value claiming are linked parts of negotiation. Both processes are present. No matter how much creative problem-solving enlarges the pie, it still must be divided; value that has been created must be claimed." See D. A. Lax and J. K. Sebenius, *The Manager as Negotiator* (New York: Free Press, 1987), 33.

7. William Zartman and Maureen Berman proposed that negotiations proceed through three stages: the diagnostic phase, the formula phase, and the detail phase. See I. W. Zartman and M. Berman, *The Practical Negotiator* (New Haven, CT: Yale University Press, 1982).

8. See Raiffa, *The Art and Science of Negotiation.*

9. For an in-depth discussion of value-claiming tactics in negotiation, see chapter 2 of Lax and Sebenius, *The Manager as Negotiator.*

10. This term is used by Lax and Sebenius: "Where different interests are bundled into a negotiation, a good strategy can be to unbundle and seek creative ways to dovetail them." *The Manager as Negotiator,* 94. For a more detailed discussion of unbundling, see chapter 5 of Lax and Sebenius.

11. See D. A. Lax and J. K. Sebenius, "Thinking Coalitionally: Party Arithmetic, Process Opportunism and Strategic Sequencing," in *Negotiation Analysis,* ed. H. P. Young (Ann Arbor: University of Michigan Press, 1991). See also J. K. Sebenius, "Sequencing to Build Coalitions: With Whom Should I Talk First?" in *Wise Choices: Decisions, Games, and Negotiations,* eds. R. J. Zeckhauser, R. L. Keeney, and J. K. Sebenius (Boston: Harvard Business School Press, 1996). For a fascinating discussion of the relationship between issue sequencing and coalition formation, see W. H. Riker, *The Art of Political Manipulation* (New Haven, CT: Yale University Press, 1986).

Chapter 2

1. This model accounts for both the impact of structure on process and the impact of process on structure. An earlier version of this model is presented in M. Watkins, "Shaping the Structure of Negotiations," Program on Negotiation Monograph M98-1, Program on Negotiation at Harvard Law School, 1998. Walton, McKersie, and Cutcher-Gershenfeld developed a related framework, analyzing negotiation in terms of forces shaping negotiators' choices and an interaction system consisting of strategies, processes, and structures. See R. Walton, R. McKersie, and J. Cutcher-Gershenfeld, *Strategic Negotiations: A Theory of Change in Labor-Management Relations* (Boston: Harvard Business School Press, 1994). Sebenius analyzed negotiation in terms of structure, people, and context, as well as barriers and opportunities for creating and claiming value. See J. Sebenius, "Introduction to Negotiation Analysis: Structure, People, and Context," Note 896-034 (Boston: Harvard Business School, 1996).

Chapter 3

1. The focus on barriers to agreement in negotiation was inspired by Kenneth Arrow, Robert Mnookin, Lee Ross, Amos Tversky, and Robert Wilson, eds., *Barriers to Conflict Resolution* (New York: W. W. Norton, 1995), an important cross-disciplinary examination of reasons why conflicts persist. Sebenius has analyzed negotiation in terms of structure, people, and context, as well as barriers and opportunities for creating and claiming value.

2. This conceptual framework was originally presented in M. Watkins and K. Lundberg, "Getting to the Table in Oslo: Driving Forces and Channel Factors," *Negotiation Journal* 14, no. 2 (April 1998).

3. See C. W. Moore, *The Mediation Process* (San Francisco: Jossey-Bass, 1996). See also J. Bercovitch and J. Z. Rubin, *Mediation in International Relations: Multiple Approaches to Conflict Resolution* (London: Macmillan, 1992); and M. Watkins and K. Winters, "Intervenors with Interests and Power," *Negotiation Journal* 13, no. 2 (1997).

4. For a detailed discussion of differences as a potential source of joint gains, see chapter 5 of J. K. Sebenius, *Negotiating the Law of the Sea* (Cambridge, MA: Harvard University Press, 1984); and chapter 5 of D. A. Lax and J. K. Sebenius, *The Manager as Negotiator* (New York: Free Press, 1987).

5. Walton and McKersie originally observed that a tension often arose when negotiators engaged in mixed-motive negotiations: "At virtually every turn the negotiator finds himself in a dilemma: Should he conceal information in order to make his tactical commitment more credible, or should he reveal information in order to pursue integrative bargaining; should he bring militant constituents into the session to affirm feeling, or should he use small subcommittees in which new ideas can be quietly explored, etc." See R. E. Walton and R. B. McKersie, *A Behavioral Theory of Labor Negotiations: An Analysis of a Social Interaction System* (New York: McGraw-Hill, 1965), 183. Lax and Sebenius placed this strategic tension between value creating and value claiming at the heart of negotiation. See "The Negotiators' Dilemma," chapter 2 of Lax and Sebenius, *The Manager as Negotiator.*

6. See R. Putnam, "Diplomacy and Domestic Politics: The Logic of Two-Level Games," *International Organizations* 42, no. 3 (1988): 427–460. See also chapter 17 of Lax and Sebenius, *The Manager as Negotiator.*

7. The principal-agent problem is discussed in Arrow et al., eds., *Barriers to Conflict Resolution*, chapter 1. See also J. W. Pratt and R. J. Zeckhauser, eds., *Principals and Agents: The Structure of Business* (Boston: Harvard Business School Press, 1985).

8. Walton and McKersie, *A Behavioral Theory of Labor Negotiations*, proposed a model of intraorganizational negotiation and discussed interactions between internal and external negotiations in chapters 8 and 9. "The organizations participating in labor negotiations usually lack internal consensus about the objectives they will attempt to obtain from negotiations . . . Generally these internal conflicts must be resolved during the process of negotiation with the other party . . . These two processes—inter-group and internal consensus—are not always mutually facilitative. In fact, more often they are the opposite: a tactic which brings about internal consensus may not be instrumental for distributive bargaining; behavior which resolves internal conflict may not be consistent with the requirements of integrative bargaining; and so on" (p. 281–282). Putnam, "Diplomacy and Domestic Politics," analyzed the dynamics of these interactions as "two-level games." See also G. T. Allison, *Essence of Decision: Explaining the Cuban Missile Crisis* (Boston: Little, Brown, 1971); and chapter 17 of Lax and Sebenius, *The Manager as Negotiator*.

9. For an extensive discussion of bureaucratic politics and its impact on decision making, see Allison, *Essence of Decision;* see also F. C. Iklé, *How Nations Negotiate* (Millwood, NY: Kraus, 1964).

10. As Howard Raiffa, one of the founders of the field of negotiation analysis, once noted, "Significant conceptual complexities arise when even a single new party is added to two-party negotiations: coalitions . . . can now form." H. Raiffa, *The Art and Science of Negotiation* (Cambridge, MA: Belknap Press of Harvard University Press, 1982), 257.

11. See D. A. Lax and J. K. Sebenius, "Thinking Coalitionally: Party Arithmetic, Process Opportunism and Strategic Sequencing," in *Negotiation Analysis*, ed. H. P. Young (Ann Arbor: University of Michigan Press, 1991).

12. Ibid.

13. See D. Krackhardt and J. R. Hanson, "Informal Networks: The Company Behind the Chart," *Harvard Business Review,* July–August 1993. See also R. B. Cialdini, *Influence: The Psychology of Persuasion* (New York:

William Morrow, 1993). Chapter 6 is an excellent introduction to the psychology of interpersonal persuasion, exploring such processes as consistency and commitment.

14. See J. K. Sebenius, "Sequencing to Build Coalitions: With Whom Should I Talk First?" in *Wise Choices: Decisions, Games, and Negotiations,* eds. R. J. Zeckhauser, R. L. Keeney, and J. K. Sebenius (Boston: Harvard Business School Press, 1996).

15. In the words of Owen Harries, "Preaching to the converted, far from being a superfluous activity, is vital. Preachers do it every Sunday. The strengthening of the commitment, intellectual performance, and morale of those already on your side is an essential task, both in order to bind them more securely to the cause and to make them more effective exponents of it." See O. Harries, "A Primer for Polemicists," *Commentary* 78, no. 3 (1984): 57–60.

16. These ideas are developed in M. Watkins and S. Passow, "Analyzing Linked Systems of Negotiations," *Negotiation Journal* 12 (1996). A set of discrete (or separable) negotiations (N_1, N_2, N_3 . . . N_m) is a linked system when:

- Each negotiation in the system is linked to at least one other negotiation.
- Two negotiations are linked when the behavior of at least one negotiator in one of the negotiations is materially influenced by the simple existence of the other negotiation, or by events or outcomes in other negotiations.

Linkages between negotiations are either enacted by the *parties* within the system or imposed on them by forces external to the system, such as laws, customs, organizational procedures, preexisting relationships, and resource constraints.

Chapter 4

1. Kurt Lewin, a pioneer in the field of group dynamics, proposed a model of social change based on the idea of driving and restraining forces. One of Lewin's fundamental insights is that human collectives—including groups, organizations, and nations—are social systems that exist in a state of tension between forces pressing for change and forces resist-

ing change: "[The behavior of a social system is] . . . the result of a multitude of forces. Some forces support each other, some oppose each other. Some are driving forces, others restraining forces. Like the velocity of a river, the actual conduct of a group depends upon the level . . . at which these conflicting forces reach an equilibrium." K. Lewin, *Field Theory in Social Science; Selected Theoretical Papers* (New York: Harper & Row, 1951) 173.

2. R. Fisher, *International Conflict for Beginners* (New York: Harper and Row, 1970).

3. See P. N. Johnson-Laid, *Mental Models* (Cambridge, MA: Harvard University Press, 1983).

4. See E. Goffman, *Frame Analysis: An Essay on the Organization of Experience* (Cambridge, MA: Harvard University Press, 1974).

5. See K. L. Valley and A. T. Keros, "It Takes Two: Improvisation in Negotiation," draft working paper, Harvard Business School, Boston, 2000.

6. See Robert J. Robinson, "Errors in Social Judgment: Implications for Negotiation and Conflict Resolution, Parts 1 and 2," Notes 897-103 and 897-104 (Boston: Harvard Business School, 1997).

7. For a discussion of anchoring, see chapter 4 of M. H. Bazerman and M. A. Neale, *Negotiating Rationally* (New York: Free Press, 1992).

8. See chapter 11 of H. Raiffa, *The Art and Science of Negotiation* (Cambridge, MA: Belknap Press of Harvard University Press, 1982).

9. See chapter 4 in P. G. Zimbardo and M. R. Leippe, *The Psychology of Attitude Change and Social Influence* (New York: McGraw-Hill, 1991).

Chapter 5

1. Sun Tzu, *The Art of War,* Special Edition (El Paso, TX: El Paso Norte Press, 2005), 11.

2. M.Watkins, M. Edwards, and U. Thakrar, *Winning the Influence Game: What Every Business Leader Should Know About Government* (Hoboken, NJ : John Wiley & Sons, 2001), 58.

3. M. Mitchell, *Propaganda, Polls, and Public Opinion* (Englewood Cliffs, NJ: Prentice-Hall, 1970), 111.

Chapter 6

1. See G. Klein, *Sources of Power: How People Make Decisions* (Cambridge, MA: MIT Press, 1999).

2. The role of pattern recognition and mental simulation in making expert judgment possible is developed in detail in Klein, *Sources of Power.*

3. See C. R. Christensen, "Premises and Practices of Discussion Teaching," in *Education for Judgment: The Artistry of Discussion Leadership,* eds. C. R. Christensen, D. A. Garvin, and A. Sweet (Boston: Harvard Business School Press, 1991).

4. The idea of reflection-in-action as a hallmark of expertise is developed in detail in D. A. Schön, *The Reflective Practitioner: How Professionals Think in Action* (New York: Basic Books, 1983).

5. G. Klein, *Sources of Power: How People Make Decisions* (Cambridge: MIT Press, 1998), 42.

6. Ibid, p. 42.

7. Polanyi developed the distinction between tacit and explicit knowledge and the notion of interpretative frameworks for making sense of experience. See M. Polanyi, *Personal Knowledge: Toward a Post-Critical Philosophy* (Chicago: University of Chicago Press, 1958).

8. See R. Aiello and M. Watkins, "The Fine Art of Friendly Acquisition," *Harvard Business Review,* November–December 2000, 100–107.

Recommended Reading

Start by reading a good textbook on negotiation to get an overview of the field. I recommend:

Lewicki, Roy. *Essentials of Negotiation*. Alexandria, VA: Society for Human Resource Management, 2005. (This is the most recent edition.)

Then read the "accessible classics":

Carnegie, Dale. *How to Win Friends and Influence People*. New York: Simon and Schuster, 1936.

Fisher, Roger, William Ury, and Bruce Patton. *Getting to Yes: Negotiating Agreement Without Giving In*. New York: Penguin Books, 1991.

Ury, William. *Getting Past No: Negotiating with Difficult People*. New York: Bantam Books, 1991.

If you like the Fisher/Ury/Patton school of thought, take a look at related work on conflict management:

Fisher, Roger, Elizabeth Kopelman, and Andrea Kupfer Schneider. *Beyond Machiavelli: Tools for Coping with Conflict*. Cambridge, MA: Harvard University Press, 1994.

Stone, Douglas, Bruce Patton, and Sheila Heen. *Difficult Conversations: How to Discuss What Matters Most*. New York: Viking, 1999.

For an overview of "game" thinking, read:

Dixit, Avinash K., and Barry J. Nalebuff. *Thinking Strategically: The Competitive Edge in Business, Politics, and Everyday Life.* New York: Norton, 1991.

For an introduction to the analytics of negotiation, get:

Hammond, John S., Ralph L. Keeney, and Howard Raiffa. *Smart Choices: A Practical Guide to Making Better Decisions.* Boston: Harvard Business School Press, 1999.

For deeper insight, read:

Lax, David A., and James K. Sebenius. *The Manager as Negotiator.* New York: Free Press, 1987.

Raiffa, Howard. *The Art and Science of Negotiation.* Cambridge, MA: Belknap Press of Harvard University Press, 1982. (For the nonmathematically inclined, just read the first half of each chapter of this classic.)

For deeper insight into the psychology of negotiation, read:

Bazerman, Max H., and Margaret A. Neale. *Negotiating Rationally.* New York: Free Press, 1992.

Cialdini, Robert B. *Influence: The Psychology of Persuasion.* New York: Morrow, 1993.

Rubin, Jeffrey Z., Dean G. Pruitt, and Sung Hee Kim. *Social Conflict: Escalation, Stalemate, and Settlement.* New York: McGraw-Hill, 1994.

For a comprehensive look at negotiation ethics, read:

Menkel-Meadow, Carrie, and Michael Wheeler, eds. *What's Fair: Ethics for Negotiators.* San Francisco: Jossey-Bass, 2004.

If you are interested in international negotiation, read:

Brett, Jeanne M. *Negotiating Globally: How to Negotiate Deals, Resolve Disputes, and Make Decisions Across Cultural Boundaries.* San Francisco: Jossey-Bass, 2001.

Iklé, Fred Charles. *How Nations Negotiate.* New York: Praeger, 1964. (A classic in the field.)

Salacuse, Jeswald W. *Making Global Deals: Negotiating in the International Marketplace.* Boston: Houghton Mifflin, 1991.

Watkins, Michael, and Susan Rosegrant. *Breakthrough International Negotiation: How Great Negotiators Transformed the World's Toughest Post-Cold War Conflicts.* San Francisco: Jossey-Bass, 2001.

Finally, if the history of thinking about negotiation interests you, read:

Allison, Graham T. *Essence of Decision: Explaining the Cuban Missile Crisis.* Boston: Little, Brown, 1971.

Rapoport, Anatol. *Fights, Games, and Debates.* Ann Arbor: University of Michigan Press, 1960.

Schelling, Thomas C. *The Strategy of Conflict.* Cambridge, MA: Harvard University Press, 1960 (especially chapters 3 and 4).

Walton, Richard E., and Robert B. McKersie. *A Behavioral Theory of Labor Negotiation: An Analysis of a Social Interaction System.* New York: McGraw-Hill, 1965.

Index

About the Author

Michael Watkins is an expert in leadership and negotiation. He is a professor of practice at INSEAD, the leading European business school, and the founding partner of Genesis Advisers, a leadership strategy consultancy. Dr. Watkins is the author of the international bestseller *The First 90 Days: Critical Success Strategies for New Leaders at all Levels* (2003) and coauthor of *Predictable Surprises: The Disasters You Should Have Seen Coming and How to Prevent Them* (a *Strategy + Business* 2004 best business book) and of *The First 90 Days in Government* (2006). He also is the author of *Breakthrough Business Negotiation: A Toolbox for Managers* (winner of the CPR Institute prize for best negotiation book in 2002) and coauthor of *Breakthrough International Negotiation: How Great Negotiators Transformed the World's Toughest Post–Cold War Conflicts* (2001), *Winning the Influence Game: What Every Business Leader Should Know About Government* (2000), and *Right from the Start: Taking Charge in a New Leadership Role* (1999).

Dr. Watkins has designed and taught negotiation programs offered by several leading academic institutions: the Kennedy School of Government, the Harvard Business School, the Program on Negotiation at Harvard Law School, and INSEAD. He also has delivered custom negotiation programs at many leading corporations and government agencies. A native of Canada, Dr. Watkins received a degree in electrical engineering from the University of Waterloo, did graduate work at the University of Western Ontario, and completed his PhD in decision sciences at Harvard University. Between 1991 and 1996, he was a professor at Harvard's Kennedy School of Government. From 1996 to 2003, he was a professor at the Harvard Business School.